Live a Financially Healthy life

Live a Financially Healthy life

Generate income from
Different sources
Be debt free
Create wealth
Be financially secure
And retire happy

Eric Julius

iUniverse, Inc.
New York Lincoln Shanghai

Live a Financially Healthy life

Generate income from Different sources Be debt free Create wealth Be financially secure And retire happy

iUniverse books may be ordered through booksellers or by contacting:

iUniverse
2021 Pine Lake Road, Suite 100
Lincoln, NE 68512
www.iuniverse.com
1-800-Authors (1-800-288-4677)

This book contains information gathered from many sources. This book is sold with the understanding that neither the author nor the publisher is engaged in rendering financial or retirement advice.

ISBN: 0-595-33423-7 (pbk)
ISBN: 0-595-66917-4 (cloth)

Printed in the United States of America

This book is dedicated to my late father—Julius.

CONTENTS

Preface ix

Generate income from different sources 1

Income from different sources—Part II 13

Income from different sources—Part III 26

Credit Cards facts 37

Mortgages and Car Loans Facts 59

Ways you can save money 69

Be debt free 79

Gain Financial Advantage 88

Create Wealth 98

Retire Happy 118

Scams and Schemes 141

Find Free Money and Help 145

References 161

Index 165

PREFACE

This book explain the simple and in-depth Financial concepts used in America today by consumers, investors, businesses, government and Financial institutions. It is broken down into different financial needs of any individual who need to acquire wealth, protect wealth, give wealth, share wealth and control wealth. The ways we have been doing all of these had led many people in America to start suffering from Financial cancer. This is a very serious disease. You can look around you and you will see many who are mentally and financially bankrupt, their credit cards debt are way over their limits and they are behind on their mortgage payment. They have a job they are not happy with and they are scared of loosing. They don't know who and where to turn to with their problems. This book will help you to solve all these problems that have created all kinds of medical problems in some peoples' lives. All these create worries, stress and lead to high blood pressure, stomach ulcers and insomnia. In the world we live in today, being financially smart, can safe your life and your money. This book will give you a free ride to financial freedom. All you have to do is set the ball rolling and reading this book is a start. This book gives you a collection of financial expertise and knowledge right at your finger-tips. Although, live is hard, but it can be easy with the right knowledge. You can easily get to your destination the right way in this journey of life. Read on and you are on your way to acquiring financial health.

All you have to do next is to just utilize the information you acquire from this book. Believe in yourself and keep on keeping on. You may have made some mistakes in the past, but don't be too hard on your self, because you are a masterpiece. You are one and only. There is still room for you to create wealth and become financially independent. There is no one out there exactly like you. You are in this world to be financially healthy and this book will surely take you there. Be confident, assertive and resourceful, in your quest for financial health. All it really takes is good attitude and a little bit of creativity on your part. It is time you prove to the world and especially those who say you cannot be rich that you can. Be your number one fan. Even when nobody believes in you, you should believe in yourself. This book can make you live rich and die rich. This book will put money in your pocket and help you from getting ripped off.

Free yourself at Last

Yes—you are free at last from the bondage of debt and financial cancer—complete freedom is now yours. Your schedule is no longer governed by others. You can make all your decisions by yourself. No body tells you what to do and how. Where to be and when. You are no longer in that cage, you call office. Now you can do what you love and love what you do. Your days are precious currency of your life. You now have abundance in your life.

If you spend your days in unsatisfying tasks in which you feel ungratified, you are simply spinning your wheels to pay bills. You are working to satisfy something outside of you—which is financial obligations. If you believe in abundance instead of scarcity you will find a way to do what you love rather that settling due to lame excuses—like you don't have enough to do what you would like to do or you have no choice—These, all indicate scarcity of what you need to survive. And you feel forced. It is not supposed to be so.

GENERATE INCOME FROM DIFFERENT SOURCES

Supplementing your Income

Generating income apart from your regular job can also come from interest earned, dividends, rents and little side businesses. For example: dividends on corporate stocks, interest on municipal or government/corporate bonds, rent from real estate. It can simply be interest from savings or money-market account. This kind of income is referred to as **return** or **yield**. The return is in dollars while the yield is in percentages. If your money-market account has 3-percent annual yield, the accumulated interest is what you actually get in addition to what you put there. It is also true in case of dividends, because it is the additional income you receive.

Look at your supplemental income generation in three areas.

o   To protect your capital:—like savings accounts, money markets, EE/HH bonds etc.

o   To provide you with income:—like stocks that pay regular dividends and rental property.

o   To give you growth in dollar value:—like growth stocks and undeveloped real estate like land.

One paycheck may not cut it

Actors, musicians, and many entertainers have residual income, which is the best kind of income and they also do many things to generate income from different sources. Some of the musicians are movie stars, TV actors, they own clothing lines and restaurants, and these kinds of businesses have repeat customers. We all know that these days, one paycheck does not cut it in most cases. Even some two income families are striving to pay their bills. Moreover, there is no longer job security and the only security these days is you. Jobs have become temporary. "Security resides in the person, not the job....Find your security from within, not from without." Measure your self-worth not base on your job but on yourself. Think of yourself as a masterpiece and priceless individual.

Corporations don't care about you; all they care about is what they can suck out of you. If anything doesn't go their way, you are sacked. Don't be too comfortable with the rat race, even if you are winning the rat race. Who have you seen in their dying bed; say "I wish I would have spent more time at the office?"

Residual versus Linear income.

Residual income is very smart money and there are many ways you can earn it. **Residual income is** also called passive or recurring income—that is income that continues to be generated after the initial effort has been expended. Compare this to what most of us focus on earning: linear income, which is one-shot compensation or payment in the form of a fee, wage, commission or salary from whatever you do.

Linear income is directly proportional to the number of hours expended (40 hours of pay for 40 hours of work). One of the great advantages of residual income is that once things are set in motion, you continue making money from your initial efforts, while gaining time to devote to other things in many other areas—such as generating more streams of residual income!

There are a variety of ways residual income can be earned.

Following are some examples.

1. The rights to a book you wrote, a software program you created, a gadget you invented, or a song you recorded, to a company that agrees to pay you a percentage of each copy of your work sold in the future.

2. Transfers from the Video games, Paintings, sculptures, photographs, and architectural designs.

3. An actor draws residual income from each of their movies, TV shows, or commercials, each time they run.

4. If you let oil company drill a well on your property in exchange for a percentage of the revenue.

5. If you purchase an office building or other real estate that earns you recurring income through lease or rental payments.

The above ways of earning residual income generally aren't that easy to implement.

Following are some that are more attainable for the average person:

6. Maintain a savings and investment program that pays you residual income in the form of interest or dividends.

7. Market your own products and/or services that lend themselves to repeat sales.

In a nutshell you should focus on products or services that are regularly used or consumed, and that must be purchased over and over again. A product or service that you create once, but sell over and over again, is easily categorized as a form of residual income

There are three major types of incomes

• Earned income

• Passive income

• Portfolio income

Earned Income

This kind of income is the income you get from your employer. If you work for a corporation, you are getting earned income. It could be salary, contract employee pay, commission employee pay etc. This is the worst kind of income in the income category. You can fight from the inside and you can fight from the outside to get earned income. Fighting from the inside here is being an employee and doing what an employee does to make ends meet. You can also fight from the outside without being controlled and you make full decisions regarding your future income and investments. These are like Doctors and Lawyers. Doctors and Lawyers earn linear income because they can only serve a certain number of people at one time in a day. There is cap on their income potential.

Passive Income

These are income you generate from business or businesses that you own. This is the best kind of income because if you work hard, it will surely pay off in the long run. Many people work hard as employee and get laid off through downsizing. While in this bracket, many people find themselves working less and less as time progresses. This kind of income can help you to retire early. What I mean by retirement here is the fact that your day to day activities will not be dictated and regulated by someone other than customers. You wake up when you think is appropriate and do what you love to do. Most people work hard all their lives with little or nothing to show for it. If you have your own business, your money can really work for you.

Passive income is very good income because it is one of the areas the rich generate and park their money. This is very good mostly because it can help you to payless taxes, especially when you reinvest your profits. These are monies that are generated by many businesses; it could be a full time or part time business. Most of this income does not have any cap on the income potential.

- Passive income comes mostly from your single level business or marketing. For example, most businesses and business people have this kind of income.

- Residual income (passive income) comes from a multi-level marketing that is involve in making money through single level marketing by sponsoring new direct sellers.

Single-level business or marketing is when one is making money by serving/producing or buying products from a parent company and then selling or servicing those products directly to customers.

Portfolio Income

You generate this type of income by putting your money in an investment vehicle and wheel that suits you. In this case, your money will work for you rather than you working for your money. Apart from owning businesses, the rich generate a lot of income from their portfolios. The conservative portfolio investors protect their principals and most of them do not play the stock market game. They build their wealth without the Wall Street. The conservative style in most cases is risk free and can give a bit more return than the regular savings account. Portfolio income is very good source of income because you can defer taxes on 100 percent of your investment profits. In this case, you can withdraw your principal. If the taxes are too much, you can get a policy loan and your loan will not be taxed.

- Portfolio income comes from investment mostly from trading securities like stocks, bonds and other paper assets. For example, professional traders.

Strategy number one—Conservative

Source 1: Savings Account

Some conservative investors still use this kind of account not only to pack their monies, but actually they get good interest out of it. You can research interest rates at bankrate.com. INGDirect.com gives a very good return on this kind of account with their orange savings account. Take for example; if you put in $50 in every pay period, like most people who are paid every two weeks, at the end of the month, you will be able to put in $100. At the end of the year, you will be surprise to find out that you have $1,200 in a good interest generating account. i.e. $1200 divided by 12 = $100. If you only want to save $1000 a year, you can put in $83.33 a month i.e. $83.33 multiply by 12. You will be surprised that if you keep it up by the end of five years, you will have between $5000 or $6000, it depends on your choice, plus interest. Slow and steady they say win the race. Although most people now use their savings accounts at most banks to hedge bounce checks from their checking account i.e. Overdraft protection, which is better than line of credit—that is interest based loan. Shopping around for a savings account as part of your investment vehicles should not be overlooked.

Source 2: Certificate of deposit

You can invest a minimum of $500 for a period of time with a fixed interest. In most cases, it will be 6 months, 1 year, 2 years and so on. The best way to make good money out of this kind of investment is to ladder your CD by buying different maturity dates. The advantage is that laddering of the CD's will help you to maintain liquidity and minimize exposure to interest rate swings. For example, if you have $5000, you can buy a

- $1000 CD that will mature in five years at 5.75 interests.
- $1000 CD that will mature in four years at 5.00 interests.
- $1000 CD that will mature in three years at 4.75 interests.
- $1000 CD that will mature in two years at 4.00 interests.
- $1000 CD that will mature in one year at 2.75 interests.

This will help you to have money available every year and still get the five year interest rate. If you cannot wait this long, you can start with short term ladder of three months to one year. You have to be careful for the penalty for early withdrawal. It can really cost you.

6.25	Put $1000 from 2005 here and so on-upward.	2010
5.75	$1000	2009
5.00	$1000	2008
4.75	$1000	2007
4.00	$1000	2006
2.75	$1000	2005

Source 3: Money market deposit account

This kind of account is a savings account that is federally insured, with limited check-writing privileges. You can get money from this type of account whenever you want the money with a penalty. Some banks may impose a monthly fee and you could be limited to a fixed number of transactions each month You should shop around for this kind of account at most banks, credit union and savings and loans institutions. The easiest place to start is—bankrate.com. This is where you can pack monies you may need in the near future, like home down payment. In this type of account, my favorite is the one that is tied to the movement of the prime rate. You can direct deposit your pay into this account and transfer the money you need to your regular checking account. You can accumulate good interest from this account, for example if you use virtual-bank.com's emoney account or check for other interest rates at bankrates.com.

GOVERNMENT OR TREASURY SECURITIES

T-bills, T-notes and T-bonds are higher-yield money-market securities, because they are financial obligations of the Federal governments. If you buy treasury securities from a broker or financial institution, you will pay a sales fee. But if you buy it directly from a Federal Reserve office or branch, you will pay no sale fee. The Federal Reserve Bank system has 12 regional offices: Atlanta, Boston, Chicago, Cleveland, Dallas, Kansas City, Minneapolis, New York, Philadelphia, Richmond, San Francisco and St. Louis. There are 29 state branches. Call your local branch and request for the "Federal Note Announcement"—This will give you notice of when Treasury securities will be auctioned. Check with your local bank or Federal Reserve Bank. You can buy them in person or by mail.

Source 4a: U.S.Treasury Bills

T-bills were popular before Mutual Funds and the interest reached double digits in the 80's. They are sold or offered for 13, 26 or 52 weeks. If you buy a 26
week T-bill for $1000, you will immediately receive a check of $300, it depends
on the interest rate. This is if it is 6%. You will receive a check for $1000 the
original amount you invested after six months or you may choice to reinvest it.
This investment is made with the Federal Government as such you will pay
federal taxes on the interest you received, but you will not pay State taxes.

Source 4b: T-notes

These government securities can mature in 2 to 10 years. T-notes have a minimum face value amount of $5000.

Source 4c: T-bonds

The T-bonds start at a face value of $1,000. They mature in 10 to 30 years.

*Note: You should know the difference between money market deposit fund and money
market mutual fund before investing in a money market account.*

Source 5: Money market Mutual Fund

This kind of account invests in short term debt instruments such as U.S.
Treasury bills and top-rated corporate debt. Start at bankrate.com when shopping around for this kind of investment.

The disadvantage of this investment:

- These funds earn variable interest.
- Expenses can eat up the yield of the fund
- This kind of fund does not guarantee your principal.

Source 6: Mutual Funds

Mutual funds are not federally insured, maybe the portfolio has guaranteed
securities or the funds may have private insurance protection.

- Mutual funds pool money together from many investors to buy stocks,
  bonds and other securities or a mixture of both.
- Within the mutual funds family, don't be confused with stock funds and
  bond funds.

- Stock funds are mutual funds whose holdings consist mainly of stocks. There are different types of stock funds:
    o   Aggressive growth
    o   Growth and income funds
    o   Balance stock funds
    o   International general
    o   International regional
    o   Global stock funds
    o   Sector stock funds etc
- Bond funds are mutual funds whose holdings consist mainly of bonds. There are many different types of bond funds:
    o   Investment grade
    o   High-yield corporate
    o   High-yield munis etc

You should find out as much as possible before investing in any mutual fund. You can easily do this at your bank, financial institutions, and brokerage firms and better yet over the internet, like at—www.ici.org or www.fidelity.com. "Mutual Funds are long-term investments and shouldn't be judge on short-term performance."

Find out more about a fund at:

www.personalwealth.com

www.morningstar.net

There is no such thing as a free lunch

—Milton Friedman

The classes of funds

1. **Class A shares:** It charge "front-end" sales load, so investors pay this at the time of purchase. The fee can be as high as 8.5 percent of the assets. Although in most cases, they are between 3 to 6 percent. "Investors purchasing large amounts may reach a "breakpoint" in sales charges—as sales increase over a specified dollar amount, the load decreases."

2. **Class B shares:** This have a contigent deferred sales charge, called "rear-end" or "back-end" load. Some of the funds out there provide service or option to allow investors to invest without upfront fees. The fees in this class of funds are highest for those who sell shares soon after purchasing them; they decline as time goes on, usually from 5% to 1%. This class include "12b-1" fee. The 12b-1 fee is an annual fee that ranges from 0.5 percent to more than 1 percent to compensate your financial advisor for monitoring your funds.

3. **Class C shares:** They are also called "level load." This include a 1 percent contigent deferred sales charge on shares redeemed within approximately 1 year of purchase, but not more than 13 months. If you plan to hold a fund for a short period, this may be the least expensive way for you to go.

4. **No-Load Funds:** These are funds that charge no fee to buy or sell shares. These funds are not actually free. They charge management and transaction fees. The fees are subtracted from the fund's share price, reducing the shares' net asset value.

Source 7: Profitable Hobby

If you cannot start a business now due to financial resources or the bank will not lend you money, it is possible you have something you really enjoy doing. It could be your hobby in this case like photography, stamps collections or other collectibles. If you are knowledgeable about stamps, you can make profit trading stamps on the side as side income. You may have other profitable hobbies like acquiring collectibles like Tiffany Lamps, Coca-cola memorabilia, exotic rugs, Teddy bears, baseball cards, paintings etc. The retail prices for these collectibles are most of the time higher with time. You have to really know the products before buying. The best place to start is checking out their auctions and then belonging to their club or reading the club newsletter.

Source 8: C-Share Annuity

You can use C-share annuity to pack your money for a short period of time. This is because it gives higher interest rate than money market account. The risk is very low if you put your money in this vehicle. You can get rate of up to 5% when the money market account with most lender is still below 2%.

Strategy Two—Bonds

Facts about bonds:

* When interest rates drop—**Bond prices rise**—because you will receive more for a bond with higher interest rate.
* When interest rates rise—**Bond prices fall**—because you will receive more for a bond with a lower interest rate.

Source 9: Municipal bonds

Municipal bonds are also called Munis. They are issued by States, Cities, Counties, and local governments. "They're not always graded (or rated), but when they are, they are almost always investment grade, particularly when secured." Their yields are generally high and they are usually free of Federal taxes. In most cases, they are also free of State and local taxes, if issues by State in which you reside. You can ask at your bank or financial institution about municipal bonds or any brokerage firm and better yet go to bondpage.com

Source 10: Corporate Bonds

These bonds are issued by corporations to raise capital, just as other bonds. Corporations issues different types of bonds and they are graded on the ability of the Company to repay the bond holders. The yields on corporate bonds are paid semi-annually and they are traded frequently. "Trading is based on the price of the bond, which can fluctuate as a result of the company's financial outlook." You should carefully study the company issuing the bond. Bonds rating provide a significant indication of whether the company will default on the bonds.

Source 11: Convertible Bonds

These are corporate bonds which can be converted into shares of stock in the issuing company. This usually happen either on request or after a fixed time frame.

Source 12: Junk Bonds

This is mostly done by small companies or companies in shaky financial straits. They sell junk bonds—also known as high-yield bonds. These companies are usually new and are trying to raise money to establish themselves. Junk bonds offer high yield in return, but they are a major risk because of their greater chance of default. They do not have investment grade ratings. There are several downfalls to these kinds of bonds. Be extremely careful with these kinds of bonds.

- They can be called when the company's financial picture improves
- The company can issue bonds at lower interest rates.
- The bonds can be downgraded from low rating to an even lower rating, causing the price to drop.

Source 13: Zero Coupon Bonds

These are government bonds and they are also known as CATS, TIGER and LIONS. They do not pay interest until the bond reaches maturity. The rates in these kinds of bonds are higher, but it takes a lot of patient to wait until maturity. Some people can buy these kinds of bonds for future expenditure, like money to buy a home or pay for child college tuition.

I, EE & HH Bonds are all different SAVINGS BONDS

Source 14a: I-Bonds

Inflation index savings bonds are issued by the U.S Treasury. I-bonds are sold at face value. For example you pay $50 for a $50 bond. The earning rates are adjusted semiannually—May and November. They are a combination of fixed interest rate plus the rate of inflation. You can invest between $50 to $30,000 per year. Check with your banks, credit union, savings and loan institutions. You can also invest by yourself over the internet at www.savingsbond.gov.

The Federal taxes on earnings can be deferred up to thirty years. You are also exempt from paying state and local taxes on this investment. You can use this to:

- Finance child education
- Supplement retirement income
- Give as a gift to your love one or organization.

Note: When inflation goes up, the interest rate decreases, but your principal is safe.

- Minimum term of ownership: 1 year
- Interest-earning period: 30 years it will continue to yield interest
- Early redemption penalties:
- Before 5 years, forfeit 3 most recent months 'interest
- After 5 years, no penalty

Source 14b: EE Bonds

The **paper type of EE bond** is issued at half their face value or par value (paper EE bonds). For example, a $1000 bond on face value is purchased at $500 for paper EE bond at your banks or financial institutions. **The electronic type of EE bond** is same amount of the bond, like $50 for $50. The interest will accrue over a period of time. This is very good for future financial planning like college saving account A very good alternative to college IRA or 529. A tax free investment, even if you choice not to use the money for your child's education. You get the face value after many years and you may lose some interest if you bail out earlier than the specified time. Check www.treasurydirect.gov or savingsbond.gov

"If you redeem an EE Bond after 18 months, you'll get the first 15 months of earnings, along with your original investment." "If you wait at least 5 years, you will not lose any interest."

Source 14c: HH Bonds

Series HH bonds are interest paying bonds that mature in ten years. These savings bonds can be held in denominations ranging from $25 to $1000. It can yield interest for up to 20 years. You can also buy this at savingsbond.gov.

"HH/H Bonds cannot be redeemed directly at a financial institution. When redeeming your HH/H Bonds, keep in mind the following:

- HH bonds must be at least 6 months old.
- You must be able to identify yourself as the owner, co-owner, or other person authorized to cash the bonds.
- The financial institution must guarantee your signature on the back of the bonds, once you establish your identity. Payment for redeemed HH/H Bonds is done via direct deposit (electronic transfer of funds into a designated account at a financial institution)."

INCOME FROM DIFFERENT SOURCES— PART II

Warren Buffets Two rules of investing:
Rule #1. Never lose money.
Rule #2. Never forget rule #1

Strategy three—Stocks

Source 15: Stocks

A company usually sells shares of its stock to help raise equity to operate the company and in turn grow the company. They anticipate both growth and profit. Those profits will be reflected in the activity of the stock and those who have invested (own shares) will be along for the ride.

Common stocks fall into several categories including blue chip stocks, growth stocks, income stocks, and cyclical stocks.

1. **Blue chip stocks:** "These are issued by companies such as IBM, Procter and Gamble, Disney etc. They have market capitalization in billions. Such prestigious established companies have solid reputation. And most of these companies have been around for over 25 years and they show no sign of slowing down."

2. **Cyclical stocks:** "These are stocks of companies whose earnings are most closely tied to the business cycle. As the economy fluctuates, these stocks will move up or down along with it. Stocks in automobiles, such as General Motors, for example, will be cyclical because when the economy is bad, fewer people will buy new cars, and when the economy is good, car buying will be up. Companies that make products such as food are not cyclical since food is a constant in any economy. Stocks for which there is consistent demand, regardless of the economic climate, are non-cyclical."

3. **Growth stocks:** "These stocks, as the name suggests, are issued by companies that are looking to grow and expand. You may be on a roller-coaster ride with such a company at the outset, but if their prognosis is correct, they will grow successfully over a period of time."

4. **Income Stocks** can give you a fixed income. There are different types of **income stocks.** Many are considered safer stocks, or less of a risk. They pay steady dividends because they are issued by long-term well established companies, rather than new comers. **Utility** companies and some **energy** companies, usually fall in this category. Anyone can buy stocks. Evaluate the company you are interested in buying and try to determine the outlook for the future, based on their past track record, their current stability, their future plans and goals. You can easily buy stocks by setting up an account with a discount brokerage firm and some of them you can open with $500 or less. The commissions they charge are very reasonable compare to full service brokerage firms.

For example, 100 shares of XYZ Company, listed at $20 on the stock exchange would cost $2000. Selling those same shares at $27 would bring you $2700 or a profit of $700.

Auto-Trade your Stocks and Options

You can **Auto-Trade** both stocks and options. One of my best advisors is http://www.schaeffersResearch.com. You can open an account with a discount trading site like http://investrade.com/ or http://www.optionsexpress.com. They will auto-trade for you and you don't have to worry when to get in and get out of the ride. Some fund manager trade your 401k and mutual funds accounts, why not stocks and options. If you are good in stocks picking, you do it yourself, but you might want to worry less and concentrate on your normal job or employment. Moreover, you don't want your boss or supervisor to catch you trading on company time. And if the market is not going your way, it can increase your blood pressure and affect your job performance. Let the people who watch the market day and night for years do it for you.

Do not catch a falling dagger, buy high and sell higher

Dollar-cost averaging

Dollar-cost averaging is a strategy for investing a set amount of money on a regular schedule, regardless of the share price at the time. In the long run, dollar cost averaging results in you accumulating more shares for low prices than you do at high prices. If you are going to buy stocks, make sure you buy **blue chip** stocks—These are stocks from companies that have been around for years.

Dollar cost Average Advantage

Date	$ Amount	Share Price	Number of shares purchased	Total dollar invested	Shares Owned	Account Value
Jan	$500	$21.00	23.81	$500	23.81	$500
Apr	$500	$21.00	23.81	$1,000	47,62	$1,000
Jul	$500	$20.00	25.00	$1,500	72.62	$1,452.40
Oct	$500	$18.00	27.78	$2,000	100.40	$1,807.20
Jan	$500	$16.00	31.25	$2,500	131.65	$$2,106.40
Apr	$500	$15.00	33.33	$3,000	164.98	$2,474.70
Jul	$500	$15.00	33.33	$3,500	198.31	$2,974.65
Oct	$500	$18.00	27.78	$4,000	226.09	$4,069.62
Jan	$500	$20.00	25.00	$4,500	251.09	$5,021.80
Apr	$500	$22.00	22.73	$5,000	273.82	$6,024.04
Jul	$500	$26.00	19.23	$5,500	293.05	$7,619.30
Oct	$500	$28.00	17.86	$6,000	310.91	$8,705.48

Without Dollar Cost Advantage

Date	Number of shares Purchased	Share price	$ Amount	Total $ Invested	Shares Owned	Account Value
Jan	25	$21	$525	$525	25	$525
Apr	25	$21	$525	$1,050	50	$1,050
Jul	25	$20	$500	$1,550	75	$1,500
Oct	25	$18	$450	$2,000	100	$1,800
Jan	25	$16	$400	$2,400	125	$2,000
Apr	25	$15	$375	$2,7775	150	$2,250
Jul	25	$15	$375	$$3,150	175	$2,625
Oct	25	$18	$450	$3,600	200	$3,600
Jan	25	$20	$500	$4,100	225	$4,500
Apr	25	$22	$550	$4,650	250	$5,500
Jul	25	$26	$650	$5,300	275	$7,150
Oct	25	$28	$700	$6,000	300	$8,400

Source 16: Index Funds and Sector Funds

Index Mutual Funds are designed to mimic the movements of a particular index. For example, a fund trying to mimic the movement of S & P 500 will purchase a representative sample of companies that closely approximates the index. The index funds hardly change their holdings; they are relatively cheap to hold.

Index funds describe the total market value of a specific group of stocks.

1. Dow Jones Industrial Average is a large cap index of 30 large company industrial stocks. DIA or Diamond.

2. The S & P 500 composite is a broader large-cap index. The 500 largest stocks, which make up about 70 percent of market valuation.

3. The NASDAQ 100 composite—is a mid-cap index mostly traded these days with a ticker QQQ.

4. Russell 2000 is made up of 3000 largest stocks and minus or less the largest 1000 stocks. It is a small cap index.

Sector Funds: This kind of fund invests in a more narrow range of companies than does a conventional mutual fund. It has more risk and potential to generate capital gains. They might invest in healthcare companies, gold-mining stocks, or only in companies that are heavily involved in foreign trade, or only in companies based in a particular foreign country or region. For example, you can choose to invest in science and technology funds etc. Make sure whatever you choose, the future of that sector looks promising and it is long-term.

You can trade this easily on your own. You can find different stocks listed in different industry groups and sectors in—Investors Business Daily—Clearstation.com, bigchart.com or msn.com. Portfolio managers that manage these kinds of funds, build portfolios of the strongest stocks in these sectors.

Source 17: Growth and income mutual fund

These funds invest primarily in dividends paying stocks of growing companies. This fund has three goals:

o   The current income

o   The growth of income

o   The long term capital management

These kinds of funds have been strong performers in a market that favors "blue-chip" stocks. This is a sound choice for novice investors. When choosing this kind of funds, make sure you go with a sector with a good long-term record. The dividends and capital gains will automatically be reinvested to permit compounding of any future growth.

Source 18: Single Stock Futures

Single-stock futures, or SSF's is a new vehicle on Wall Street, it debuted on November 8, 2002. SSF's are contracting to buy or sell 100 shares of stock at 20 percent of the cost at that time of the particular stock.

Single-Stock Futures Advantages

1. **Point-for Point-Move:**—No complex mathematical formulas. If the stock goes up, your long futures position will appreciate on a point-for point basis.

2. **No premiums, and no time decay:**
    a. Unlike options, SSF's do not have a volatility component factored into the price of futures contract.
    b. Unlike options, SSF's contracts do not have a time premium built into the price of the contract.

3. **Useful in trading ranges:** A Single-stock future trader can profit in a range environment, unlike option players who need a strong directional move to realize profits.

4. **Leverage without Complexity:** What—you-see-is-what-you-get. There are no mathematical formulas, no time decay to negatively impact the shares. If the stock rises, the corresponding SSF's position will advance on a point-for-point-basis.

Who should consider SSF's

*   Those who consider options too complex, messy or mysterious.
*   Those who don't want to contend with the complex "Black-Scholes" formula required to calculate an option's price.

Source 19: Preferred Stock

A special class of stock that may have certain voting privileges; companies typically pay preferred stock holders a fixed and high dividend. The return is similar to what you may get on bond. Companies pay preferred stock dividends before they pay common stock dividends and you can convert them to common stocks after sometime.

Source 20: Short sellers

When you short a stock, you are selling stock that you do not own. This really depends on the permissions you have in your brokerage account. If you will like to do this, you should check with your brokerage firm or your broker. A short seller is not selling an option. This is mostly done by sophisticated investors. When an investor feels that a stock is trading too high and the market or the stock is about to trend downward, they will borrow someone's stocks and sell them, then pocket the money. If the stock price drop to that price, they sold the stock, the investor will buy the stock at that lower price. They pocket the different between the purchase price and sale price as profit. Take for example: A stock price is trading at $25 a share and the stock price is trending down, you short 100 shares at $25 a share. The broker will deposit this money in your account. The account where the stock was borrowed will be given IOU. When the stock price drops to $20 a share, the investor can buy the stock at $20 and then pocket the difference between the buy and sell as profit from this transaction.

Source 21: Drips or Dip

Dividend reinvestment plans or dividend investment plans are investment plans that can allow you to purchase stocks directly from a company without going through brokerage firms and paying commissions. The different is that you cannot dictate your buying price and you cannot sell in a minute like you can with a brokerage firm. You can start this plan with a small amount and add more shares, while the dividends are reinvested. This is because the company will automatically reinvest your cash dividends. You can easily set this up on your own. To start with very little amount like $100 you can go over to the internet like Yahoo, MSN, Google and type in drips. My favorite place to start finding out about which companies' that trade drips is http://www.stockselector.com/drips.asp

Source 22: International Stocks/Mutual Fund

The big reason to look beyond our borders is that international mutual funds will allow you to invest in a broad portfolio of stocks while you reduce the risk of fluctuating domestic market. The emerging nations economically, believe it or not have higher rates of growth than the U.S. Look at it this way; it is easier for a small company to grow from $1 billion to $2 billion than for a big company to grow from $10 billion to $20 billion. Southeast Asia—stock market is growing stronger every year. Japan's economy continues to recover. Europe's are outperforming many western markets. Latin America is not doing badly. Mexico is going through economic recovery. Although, most developing countries are not as stable as U.S., but as long as the country you are interested in investing have a stable and strong political and economic structure, why not? National treasury of small Taiwan is a surplus of over $80 billion, the equivalent of about $60,000 for every child, woman and man, while the United States has a deficit of about $100,000 per person.

Strategy Four—Options Trading

Source 23: Options

Buyers of options can make money in the stock market whether the market rises or falls, the tricky part is knowing ahead of time which direction the stock or the market will take.

1. **Buying call options:** An option is a contract that provides you with the right to execute a stock transaction that is to buy or sell 100 or 150 shares of stock. This right includes a specified fixed price per share that is good until a specified date in the future. Call option is an option acquired by a buyer or granted by a seller to buy 100 or 150 shares of stock at a fixed price. The value of an option is affected by movement in the stock's market value as well as by the passage of time. "When you buy a call option, you hope that the stock will rise in price and value because that will result in a corresponding increase in value for the call. If the call has more market value, it can be sold and closed at a profit, or the stock can be bought at a fixed price below the current market value. For example: If you buy a call option for $500 giving you the right to buy 100 shares at $80 per share. Before the deadline, though the stock's price rises to $95 per share. And the option now trade at $13, which equals $1300. You can sell the option to close the transaction, giving you a profit of $800. You can also have the right if you choose to buy $100 shares at $80 or 15 points below the current market value.

When you initiate buying in opening a position, which is traditional way is call Long Position, while the non-conventional way is when you open with a sell and it is called Short Position.

2. **Buying Put options:** A put option is the opposite of a call option; this is because it refers to selling rather than buying. The put contract grants its owner the right to sell 100 or 150 shares of stock in a specified company's stock. When you buy a put, it is as though someone is saying to you, "I will allow you to sell 100 or 150 shares of this company's stock, at a specified

price per share, at any time between now and a date in the future. For that privilege, I expect you to pay me a price." For example: If you buy a put option at $6 providing you with the right to sell 100 or 150 shares at $80 per share, and the stock value falls to $70 per share and the put trading at $11, which equals $1100. As the owner of a put, you have the right to sell 100 or 150 shares at fixed price of $80, which is $10 per share above the current market value, or sell the put outright for $11 with a profit of $5 equal $500. This really is a good way to make money in the market if it is going down.

If you believe the stock will go down or decrease in value, you will want to but puts or sell calls

Note: Some options have 100 shares allocated to them while some have 150 shares of the stock allocated to one option.

If you want to trade options with an adviser, I recommend SchaeffersResearch.com.

3. **Selling or writing a covered call:** The business of covered call writing is big business to sophisticated stock holders. Covered call writing is very elementary and conservative of all the strategies that an option trader uses. Because of its conservative nature, it is allowed in retirement account. You can use this strategy in you personal or retirement account to turbo charge your IRA account. The best way to look at covered call selling is like a business. The objective is for you to generate monthly cash flow. The merchandise you use to run the business is the stock that you own in your account. If you own common stock, you should be involved in covered call writing, if not, you are letting your inventory go to waste. This is because you are not opening your store for business. The most important advantage of covered call writing as an investment strategy is that it is far safer than just owning the stocks. This is because you generate an immediate cash return on your stock holdings, and the income which is the option premium that you receive, offsets the possible declines in the stock price. For example, in August, you bought 100 shares of Cisco systems stock (csco) at 13.10, and then sold (write) a csco Jan 15 call for an option premium of 1.4 against the stock position in your account. The option premium provides an immediate 10% return for a 5 month holding period. You can maximized income and minimize your portfolio risk with covered call writing.

Note: By starting out with an opening sale transaction, you are paid the premium at the time the order is placed. You will pay a purchase price later when you close the position or if the option expires worthless, you never pay at all. In that case, the entire sale premium is yours to keep as a profit.

4. **Uncovered or naked call writing**—is when you sell calls, but you do not own the stock. This has to be approved by your broker, because of the risk involve. This can also be done with put writing (selling), which is the opposite of call writing.

5. **Put writing (Selling)**: You can also produce income by selling puts. If you think that the stock will not trade above a certain price within a certain period of time, you can sell a covered put, if you own the stock and you sell uncovered put if you don't own the stock. This is how rich people make money without using their own money. For example: You sold a $45 put for $5. Your profit zone is any price above the striking price of $45. If the stock's market value falls below $45 per share, the put will be in the money. As long as the price range remains between $40 and $45 per share, the loss upon exercise is limited because the premium you received discounts your potential basis in the stock in the event of exercise. If the stock value falls below $40 per share, you will experience a loss upon exercise.

Trade Options like a professional

For your information, before you begin buying options you must decide how much of your investment portfolio to risk. Losing streaks are a fact of the game, so never put all of your capital into options. Set aside only a portion with which to speculate—10% of your portfolio is an ideal beginning maximum for most investors.

Your ability to manage your money will be the key in your profitable options trading. Every day that passes will costs you because your option could expire worthless.

Cheaper options are usually the best plays. They give you the most leverage, and the percentage returns are better, and if the market goes against you, you are risking less money. More important, you're able to spread your capital over more positions, increasing your odds of winning.

The easiest, safest and potentially most lucrative way to profit with an option is to buy. You simply pay your money (the premium) and wait to see if the stock does what you think it will: rise if you buy a call option, fall if you buy a put option. If the stock price rises above the strike price specified in your call option, you win your bet. If the stock falls below the price specified in your put option, you win your bet. If the stock does not behave the way you thought it would you lose your bet, as well as the premium you paid for your option.

Don't be dismayed by this. Even the pros only win their bets about 20% to 30% of the time when they buy cheap options.

Sticking with undervalued options gives you two advantages:

"First, you are risking less money when you buy a cheap option. It is much easier on the pocket book to lose $40 than $400 if the option expires worthless. Second, if the stock crosses the strike price (putting it "in the money") before your option expires; you not only win your bet but your percentage gains will be more than had you bought a more expensive option. Price is the key to success in the options market. When you pay too much for an option the odds are stacked against you. Finding under priced options is simple in theory but in the real world it takes an enormous amount of work."

How to Maximize your Profits

As important as selecting the right option to buy and paying the right price is knowing when and how to take profits. Most option buyers lose not because they take the wrong positions, but because they fail to take profits properly.

To make the biggest potential profit, your first objective is to protect profits, and your second objective is to hit home runs. Most important, when your option begins to profit you must be ready to act. Be alert to sell your position if the stock pulls back (if you bought a call option), or rises (if you bought a put option) 5%. And if the stock makes a sudden big move in your direction, don't get greedy. Sell your position and pocket the money. One other consideration: If your option is in the money goes past the strike price) and enters its last week before expiration, take profits. Don't wait for it to expire. As important as taking profits is cutting losses to a minimum. Losses are part of the game, and if you don't take them and move on you will soon be out of the game. Cutting losses is easy—if an option falls in value by 50% after you buy it, sell it and close your position. The harder part is convincing yourself to do it. I can't stress this enough—if you do not cut your losses quickly, you will not last as an options player. You should maintain consistency in your trades, most beginners' trade with 10% of their account.

For example below, this cheap options' trading was started with $7,500 and traded consistently with 20% of the portfolio value—at the end of six months profit = $9,747.51.

These are **in the money** options with one to two months to expiration date.
Beginning Portfolio Value = $7,500
Current Portfolio Value = $17,247.51

Cheap Options Trading

Entry Date	Position	Symbol	Entry	Exit	Accum Profit	Date Closed
11/13	Dec. 12.5 call	SUQ LV	1.500	1.000	($375.00)	11/21
11/26	Dec. 20 call	STK LD	1.325	2.800	$814.74	12/5
12/1	Dec. 20 put	AQF XD	1.150	2.400	$2,170.40	12/19
12/12	Jan. 15 put	SCH MC	1.000	0.675	$1,755.81	12/19
1/2	Jan. 15 put	AWE MC	1.075	2.225	$3,241.04	1/8
1/14	A Feb. 17.5 put	ORQ NW	1.625	1.150	$2,770.09	1/17
2/20	Mar. 17.5 put	NUL OW	1.375	0.600	$1,901.80	3/4
2/25	Mar. 42.5 put	XOM OV	1.800	0.725	$939.12	3/4
3/8	Mar. 35 put	SGP OG	1.275	1.375	$1,038.40	3/14
3/22	Jan. 30 put	OZC MD	1.625	5.200	$3,856.07	6/14
4/3	Apr. 20 put	BMC PD	1.475	2.975	$5,179.58	4/5
4/5	Apr. 42.5 call	LOW DV	1.700	2.150	$5,580.54	4/1
5/15	Jun. 17.5 put	QMN RW	1.275	2.675	$7,381.24	5/31
5/30	Jul. 22.5 put	DIS SX	1.050	2.375	$9,747.51	6/12

In this second example is QQQ index option, it was traded with 20% of $10,000 consistently. At the end of the trades the accumulated profit was $22,260.93. This was the gain in 6 months.

These are **in the money** options with one to two months to expiration date.

Beginning Portfolio Value = $10,000
Current Portfolio Value = $32,260.93

QQQ Option Trading

Entry Date	Position	Symbol	Entry	Exit	Accum Profit	Date Closed
12/20	Jan. 41 put	QQQ MO	2.775	1.375	($1,009.01)	1/3
1/31	Mar. 39 put	QQQ OM	2.200	4.400	$789.19	2/19
2/27	Mar. 36 put	QQQ OJ	2.175	1.025	($351.74)	3/4
3/6	Apr. 39 put	QQQ PM	2.875	1.975	(955.80)	3/8
3/1	Apr. 39 put	QQQ PM	2.350	4.700	(51.38)	4/5
3/18	Apr. 39 put	QQQ PM	2.350	5.550	$1,180.17	4/11
3/22	Jan. 30 put	OZC MD	1.625	5.200	$5,210.42	6/14
4/19	May. 36 put	QQQ QJ	2.025	4.200	$7,654.46	4/26

Entry Date	Position	Symbol	Entry	Exit	Accum Profit	Date Closed
4/25	Jun. 32 put	QAV RF	1.525	3.100	$10,503.95	5/3
5/20	Jun. 34 put	QAV RH	2.425	5.250	$14,519.45	6/4
6/4	Jun. 30 call	QAV FD	0.775	0.375	$12,151.33	8/19
6/11	Jul. 30 put	QAV SD	2.750	5.700	$16,661.93	7/2
7/8	Jul. 25 put	QAV SY	0.750	1.575	$19,594.74	7/10
7/8	Jul. 25 put	QAV SY	0.750	1.500	**$22,260.93**	7/15

6. **LEAPS:** Owning a LEAP is less risky than owning a stock in some ways. Leaps are options that have about two years before expiration. The amounts that the Leap changes in price when the stock falls is based on a measure called Delta value. Leaps can either be call or put options. Since many of the Leaps last more than 2 years, they are stock options with extended life. Unlike short-term options, your stock does not have to skyrocket right away for you to make money. If you purchase a call Leap option, you have plenty of time for an upswing. The downside to Leaps is that if the price of the stock remains flat, the leap decline in value every single month. This is because you own a depreciating asset, just like a car. The amount that the Leap falls in value each month is called the decay value. If you want to see most of the companies that trade Leaps, go to—http://www.terrystips.com/LEAPS

7. **Combinational Option Strategies:** Options traders use the above strategies like buying calls, buying puts, selling calls and selling puts, and some of the combinational techniques below:

   • Vertical Spread or money spread

   • Bull Spread

   • Bear spread

   • Box spread

   • Debit and credit spreads

   • Horizontal and diagonal Spreads

   • Ratio Calendar spread

   • Butterfly spread

   • Long Hedge

   • Short Hedge

   • Reverse Hedge

- Variable Hedge
- Ratio Write
- Long Straddle
- Short straddle

INCOME FROM DIFFERENT SOURCES— PART III

Strategy Five—Real Estate/properties

Source 24: Foreclosures

Foreclosure is a common term used to describe the procedure followed in enforcing a creditor's rights when a debt secured by any lien on property is in default

Tax sales is when the government offer a property for sale to satisfy a tax lien, the successful bidder buys the right to own the property if the property owner does not repay him or her (right of redemption). It is not the same with foreclosure sale, because in foreclosure, the former owner does not have the right to buy the house back like it is with tax sale.

Foreclosures are usually offered by:

1. FDIC—The Federal Deposit Insurance Corporation

2. GSA—Government Services Administration. They dispose of homes that the Federal government seizes or no longer needs.

3. IRS—Internal Revenue service—They foreclose on properties for delinquent taxes. They usually have public sale.

4. The Treasury Department—Properties that are seized by the Treasury Department for illegal activities are publicly auctioned out.

5. County real estate tax sale—is a form of foreclosure "When real estate taxes go unpaid, the county in most states sells Tax lien Certificates on the default property. These certificates are sold to investors for the amount of taxes due plus annual interest ranging from 0% to 50%." "The tax liens are usually redeemed by the property owner, but if not, the lien holder after a

stipulated length of time can foreclose on the lien and gain title to the property."

Pre-foreclosure: This has to do with when the lender files a notice of default— a notice of homeowner's failure to perform his/her obligations as to meet payments on the property. They are usually recorded in **Lis Pendens** records or files. Lis Pendens—pronounced (lease pen-dense) Latin for "a suit pending," by law dictionary means a written notice that a lawsuit has been filed which concerns the title to the real property or some interest in that property. The lis pendens (or notice of pending action) is filed with the clerk of the court, certified that it has been filed and it is recorded with the county recorder. This gives notice to the defendant who owns the real estate or rather owe on it that there is a claim on the property. This is before the general public is notified regarding the foreclosure date.

If you want to buy a pre-foreclosed property, this is when you step in, i.e. before they foreclosed on it.

Direct acquisition: Check the Lis Pendens in your local court house. You can contact the delinquent owner in many different ways, it depend on the contact information you may have. Sometimes the delinquent owner might be 3 to 6 months behind in payments. You can contact the person by

◊ Calling on the phone if you have the phone number

◊ Drive to the house if they are still there or ask the neighbors for their where about.

◊ Send a fax letter if you have their fax number

◊ Send e-mail if you have e-mail address of the owner.

◊ Write them a letter.

◊ Put a note on the mail box.

Quit Claim deed: You can try to get a quit claim deed from the owner so that he will not be foreclosed upon and his credit will not be ruined. For example, a $250,000 home with a $2,000 mortgage a month, and four months behind, can easily add up to be $12,000 or more when you include the late fee charges, collection fee and foreclosure fee. All you can do is approach the owner through your chosen media, to ask the owner to forget the amount he is in default. You can pay it to the mortgage company or with a note or some payment arrangement with the mortgage company, you can get a house that may have $50,000 equity for really nothing down and the owner's credit record is not affected by foreclosure.

Indirect acquisition: You can check with a realtor, MLS or a mortgage company and ask them if they have any pre-foreclose properties you can bid on. This is after you have been pre-approved for the loan amount. In this case, you have the opportunity of formally looking at the house before you bid on it. If you win the bid the house is yours at a great deal.

Post-foreclosure: The foreclosure itself is always done in public as auction, usually in front of the court house. If you are interested in being at the auction, find out the foreclosure dates in your county of interest. And the lists of the properties are usually made public in the court house or local paper. If it is tax sales, they are usually in the public records in the county of the property. After foreclosure, the lender, which is the bank or mortgage company, may have the property. You can always ask any bank to let you see the properties, since these properties are liabilities to the banks—every bank has a list of these properties and they are always eager to sell them. They are called R.E.O's or real estate owned or ORE which is Owned real Estate. Any banker who understands what you are asking for will share the list with you. You can find the list online in some bank's websites.

If the property is owned by tax authority and it has been through the tax foreclosure process (tax sales), you can bid on it with a letter or on the internet in some counties. You can get a property for even $50 if you are the highest bidder. These are the ways that some properties are bought for resale on eBay. It is not uncommon for a property that was bought for $50 in this manner, to sell on eBay for more than a $1,000. If you have not seen the real estate auctions on eBay, then go there and look—Just look at all of the properties that are selling for around $1,000 or more, and many of these were bought for less than $100.

You can get some foreclosed properties at <u>www.absoluteauctionhomes.com</u>— They always set the sale not to exceed—below 10% of the property tax market value.

Source 25: ARM's Fund

If you are looking for an investment that will provide you with a better yield than money market mutual fund, adjustable rate mortgage may be a good idea. These funds invest in mortgage pool. When mortgage rates rises, so is potential income from the funds. Some financial advisors recommend using them to replace lower-yielding short-term investments of one to three years. This is not a replacement for money market funds. This is because ARM's can fluctuate widely in price if there is a big change in interest rate. The interest rates increases with rising rates. A sharp hike in rates could cause sharp drop in share price. Many ARM funds are relatively new and have not been tested during periods of rapidly rising interest rates, so before you invest, carefully read the funds blue print

Source 26: REIT Funds and Municipal Mortgage REITs

REIT (Real Estate Investment Trust) funds are pool of funds from investors to invest in real estate. This is a very good investment vehicle if you know the real estate market, because this is indirect real estate ownership. Municipal Mortgage REIT's are real estate development companies that are selling shares which are secured by:

• Low-income-housing.

• New real estate construction

They use government tax free bonds to pay a higher tax free interest. You can find out about this from your bank or your brokerage firm. This investment can be safer and have better performance than stocks. If it is 16% a year in return, your money can double every five years. REIT's are to real estate what mutual funds are to stocks. REIT's can outperform the overall real estate market.

Source 27: Tax Forfeited Lands and Farmlands

There are many counties in the United States and most of these counties have quarterly or semi-annually tax forfeited land sales. In these auctions, believe it or not, you can get a tax forfeited land that is worth ten thousand dollars easily for a thousand. You can turn around and sell the land for $4,000, which is still less than fifty percent of the market price. You have to check them out on the web or call any county and find out if they have tax forfeited lands to auction.

Farm Lands: You drive around some time in the rural areas and you see some abandoned farms that could be for sale. You can also check Newspapers for these kinds of lands. You can get an abandoned farm land worth $50,000 for $5,000, and then get a surveyor to divide the land, and plant some trees on the land. You can advertise the land and make a lot of money.

Source 28: Residential Real Estate Rentals: You should first and foremost, check out how much the houses are rented in the neighborhood you are interested in buying a property or the neighborhood you want to rent out a property. This is because you don't want to buy a house that you are paying $1,200 a month on mortgage while similar houses are rented for $1,000. This is appli-

cable even if it is your current house that you want to rent out and move. If you finally arrive at a very good deal with positive cash flow, you can get maintenance insurance coverage for the tenants, because you may not want them to call you in the middle of the night for you to come and fix a linking toilet. I met a landlord the other day, who told me that his tenant makes payment directly to an account he setup solely for the rental property. It sounds great. If you cannot do it this way, you can let a residential management company help you manage the property for 10% of the mortgage. You should not buy a rental property in a neighborhood that has many rental properties. You can know this when you drive around the neighborhood and see many for rent signs. This is because too much competition will affect your pricing.

Source 29: Cooperative Real Estate Ownership

This is a joint venture with your friends, associates, community members or interest group. You can collectively come up with the same amount or different amount of money to buy a property. You will then draw up an agreement with the help of a lawyer. In most cases, in these kinds of ventures, they usually buy commercial real estate properties, shopping plaza, an apartment etc. They include in their agreement how they will share the income after the expenses has been deducted. It can be done in the inner city or in rural areas.

Source 30: Tax Lien Certificates and Deeds

1. **Tax Lien certificates:** TLC are fixed income investment and are very safe. This is also very good retirement investment. This is a very big secret investment that many conservative investors have been using for years. Many people do not know about it because the banks, financial institution and brokerage firms are not allowed to buy or sell tax lien certificates. This prevents the commercialization of this investment. This is way better than Mutual funds and stock market, because your principal is protected and your interest, which is your profit, is guaranteed and high these certificates are sold by local governments. They generate annual interest from 10%, 20%, 30%, 40%, and even 50% in some states. Local Governments depend on taxes, including property taxes to run government and provide services. They usually find it difficult to budget or even to function, if the taxes owned are not paid on time. By purchasing the tax lien certificate. You will pay the taxes for the delinquent tax payer that owns the property. The interest that they will be charged will go to you with a specified period of time. This means that unpaid taxes become a lien on the property. The tax obligation is recorded in the government's property records, and until the

taxes are paid, the lien remains on the property. If the taxes are not paid for a long enough periods, the owner will lose the property. Meanwhile, a penalty of from 8% to 50% per year is being added to the amount of the lien. Having this kind of lien on the property, means that nobody can buy the property without being subject to the lien. Government—issued tax liens are super-safe, and they are superior to the first mortgages.

2. **Tax Deeds:** In some states, tax lien is included with the deed, while it is separate in many states. Tax deeds are also usually sold at government auctions in most cases and they are sold in different counties all across the country. The government will auction out the properties of the owner who are defaulted in paying property taxes. In some states you can get possession of the house immediately, while in others, it usually takes a year or more before you will actually acquire ownership of the property. In Georgia for example: There are Tax Deeds with hidden tax lien. "While the successful bidder receives a tax deed, he has no immediate control over the property. The taxpayer or any other person having a right, title, interest in, or lien upon the property may redeem it at any time within twelve (12) months from the date of sale by paying the redemption price. The purchaser is not entitled to rents and/or profits arising from the property during the redemption period." "The redemption price is the amount paid for the tax deed at tax sale plus any taxes subsequently paid by the tax deed purchaser plus 20% of that amount for the first year or fraction of a year elapsing between the date of the sale and the date of redemption. After the first year following the conclusion of the tax sale the tax deed purchaser is entitled to an additional 10% for each subsequent year or fraction of a year until redemption."

Source 31: Franchises

Franchising is one of the biggest secret that the rich use to generate and preserve their wealth in modern life. While the poor and middle class are working herder and harder, the rich are using this method to get richer and richer. These days, some fast food restaurants have a program that they allow their employee to own a branch. This is because it is very expensive for most people to come up with the down payment, talk less of them having good income, savings and credit to qualify. This is very easy way to generate wealth, because the business plans have already been tried and successful in the field. All you have to do is run with it. But it will cost you.

If you are interested, choose a business that you love and passionate about especially if you are the one who is going to run the business. If you are not going to run the business yourself, it does not matter whether you love the business or not, all you will be looking at is the profit. And at the end you will have money to afford not to work. Some baby boomers are now looking at this kind of option for retirement.

Triple Net Lease real estate: You should know that McDonald is not in hamburger business it is in real estate business. Kmart stock starts to bounce back after bankruptcy because of its real estate locations. This is because if you look at their locations, you will discover that the price of their lands happens to be more expensive than their business. You can buy or build in a commercial space and rent it out to one of these businesses. This is an excellent investment when a triple net lease is signed. You will be set for life. This is because:

1. Triple net lease investments are often in excellent commercial locations, such as a street corner of a busy intersection.

2. The tenant is often a public company such as major drugstore, fast food restaurant, or a national retail chain, this is going to be steady and secure cash flow.

3. The tenant is responsible for everything. It is call triple net lease because the tenant pays for

    a. Maintenance or Repairs

    b. Insurance

    c. Taxes

Strategy Six—Internet

Source 32: Internet Auction

Instead of having a garage sale, why not sell those stuffs over the internet in an auction website. You can check your garage or storage for:

*   Old Shoes
*   Used Books
*   Used Toys
*   Used Clothes
*   Jewelries
*   Kitchen goods
*   Video games
*   Gifts items

- Bags and purses

You can sell these products and more in an auction website like eBay, or even sell them at Amazon.com website.

Source 33: E-commerce and Affiliate programs

If you have a product to sell or a service idea, you want to first and foremost look into an e-commerce website, because it will be cheaper to maintain than a traditional store front. In most cases these days companies try out their product ideas on the internet storefronts before they physically take them to the traditional stores. Take for example, Amazon.com was just a concept that Jeff Benzoe took to Seattle from Wall Street were he was working because the internet usage was growing at an alarming rate. The internet sale for 2004 is in billions and still growing. In fact, the internet forces many businesses to close their doors. In the future, it is going to force some banks to close their doors as more and more customer's use internet banking and ATM. This is because if you look around, you will find better rate or return for your money with internet banking that the traditional banking businesses. You can advertise in some E-zines to help you drive traffic to your website. E-zines are internet magazine or newsletters.

Affiliate Programs: If you cannot afford to set up your own web site, you can affiliate your self or your business with the big companies. They can set up a website for you for free or just for a little monthly payment. In fact, some people are making a lot of money by owning these kinds of websites.

Source 34: Direct Marketing

Direct marketing is big business, believe it or not. Many people are making millions from direct marketing. Direct marketing can now be done

- Over the internet
- Newspapers and magazines
- Sending letters and postcards
- Phone calls with good marketing pinch.

If you have a good idea or product to sell, this is a very good source to reach your potential customers. "Knowing how to write ads and where to place them is the real secret to mail-order marketing success." Using the right word that catches the reader's eyes and ears. Most people who are successful in this kind of business have a lot of time and financial freedom.

Strategy Seven—HARD ASSETS

Source 35: Silver and Diamond

This is an anti-inflationary traditional investment. People turn to this hard asset in times of war, political unrest and when prices of goods and services are rapidly rising. Although, silver may tarnish, but not speculative as gold. You can buy

- The pure-silver coins
- Silver—mine shares
- Silver futures
- Precious-metal mutual funds.

Be careful, because many Gold funds also invest in silver shares. Watch out if you are trying to invest in gemstones. The most common investment-grade stone—is the diamond.

Diamonds are difficult to evaluate, as such most people depend on reliable dealers. And since this is a very speculative area and perhaps only 1% of quality grades appreciate dramatically.

Follow these guidelines if you want to invest in diamonds.

1. You should buy very fine diamonds of half-carat to two carat sizes. These are more liquid. Buy the highest—clarity grade, using the Gemological Institute of America's grading criteria.

2. Deal only with established companies in diamond industry. You can check the company references with the Jewelers Board of Trade (Providence, RI) and Jewelers Vigilance Committee—New York City and with your local Better Business Bureau.

3. You can only buy from companies that offer a buyback guarantee in the event the diamond did not meet the specifications under which it was sold. Before you buy, get full disclosure of initial purchase fees and in writing, the fees required to resell the diamond in the future.

Source 36: GOLD

People turn to gold as the best investment to protect their real worth during war, political unrest and inflation. During crisis, it is so scarce, the price goes up. It means that small amount of gold can represent a large fortune, which is why gold is favored by wealthy people who have to flee their homelands. Gold is easily divisible and widely accepted as a form of payment. Gold is enduring popularity, because it is beautiful, malleable enough to form different decorative objects—from jewelry to statues and it is almost indestructible. Gold buying is speculative, because the prices are usually pushed by a crisis.

You can trade Gold in different valuations

1. **Gold deposit Certificates:** This kind of certificates represents an interest in gold bullion that are registered and stored in domestic or foreign banks. The return lies in the increase of gold's market price. You personally do not hold this kind of gold; as such you should buy carefully from companies that will hold it in storage. Your banker or financial adviser can refer you to a reputable dealer of Gold deposit certificates.

2. **Gold-bullion Coins:** The Canadian Maple Leaf, the South African Krugerrand, the Chinese Panda, the Mexican gold Peso, the Austrian Corona and the American Eagle are the most popular. These are commonly in one ounce and they are really valued for their gold content. Dealer commissions and markups vary—Try and shop around before buying or selling these kind of gold.

3. **GOLD Bars:** This kind of Gold is usually for large investors. This is mostly because bars must be assayed and stored with a reputable warehouse. You should only deal with companies that offer a buyback guarantee and certify the bars.

4. **Shares in Gold Mining Companies:** There are a few companies that produce mines in the United States; most of the companies you can invest in are in Canada or South Africa. You will buy the Company shares just as you buy corporate stocks. These companies may pay dividends and these shares are easy to buy and sell in the various trading markets around the World.

5. **Gold Mutual Funds:** You can buy and own shares in a fund that invests in a variety of gold stocks. This will give you mutual fund advantages like diversification, professional management, convenience and liquidity.

Source 37: Commodities Futures

The commodity speculator buys and sells contracts for future delivery of a given amount of silver, corn, grain, pork bellies, Swiss francs etc. There are about a dozen domestic commodity futures exchanges. These contracts are continuously traded, with the investor hoping that the prices for their speculated commodity move in their direction i.e. up if bought and down if sold. "If you like action and have a few thousand with which to play, then commodities market may be for you."

To buy commodities futures you will require a small margin deposit (a percentage of the contracts bought or a flat fee). The commissions and the minimum initial deposits to open a commodity account with a brokerage firm vary. The small margin allows great leverage. The trader must deposit no more than 5 to 20 percent of the value of the contract. The actual cost of the up and down fluctuations may not be noticed. For example: A contract with a value of $100,000—the trader may commit $10,000 which is 10 percent of the whole amount. If the contract increases in value by 20 percent to $120,000, the trader's profit will be $20,000 minus commissions. And that is 200 percent of the original $10,000 investment. On the flip side, if it decreases in value by 10 percent, it would wipe the trader out.

The talent for this kind of market is scarce, because predicting future price movements involves guessing at the role of the weather conditions, government intervention, consumer and farmers attitudes and other factors that can influence the supply and demand for a product.

Source 38: Currency Speculation

The speculation in the rise and fall of currency values will provide you with no dividends income or interest payments. All you are hoping for in currency speculation is—Capital gain or capital loss.

It is economic and political issues that mostly affect the up and down movement of foreign currency value.

A thorough economic and political knowledge will help the trader maximize their gain and minimize loss. The capital gain from currency speculation is taxed as ordinary income.

CREDIT CARDS FACTS

> Money is something we choose to trade our life energy for....Life energy is all we have. It is precious because it is limited and irretrievable and because our choices about how we use it express the meaning and purpose of our time here on earth.

> —Joe Dominique and Vicki Robin (Your money or your life)

Starting your credit with a credit card

Some people usually start building their credit from store credit card, because they are sometimes easy to acquire, while some people start with a bank secure credit card. If you start with a very low credit limit on the card and pay it off on time, you are on your way toward building a good credit report. If you get a higher credit limit and pay on time, you will qualify for more credit and credit cards if you apply.

In a nutshell, you can establish credit by:

1. Getting a department store or gasoline card
2. Getting a small personal loan from your bank maybe the bank require a collateral, such as a deposit into your savings account and paying it off on time making sure it is reported to credit bureaus.
3. Get a secured credit card, which is like a loan but in form of plastic instead of liquid cash or check like a traditional loan.

Secured credit cards are cards that require a deposit in advance. These cards are good for building up your credit rating. Most people start their credit by obtaining a secured credit card. They build up their credit rating with this card. Credit rating here means that you will be able to show you pay your bills on time. This is really a good starting point. Make sure you get a secured credit card from a reputable financial institution. Do not give your money to a company that may not be well known. Make sure you monitor all the terms that come with the credit card. In most cases, some papers are buried within your monthly statement, which can easily let you know the charges. You should look through these papers, because some credit cards companies use this method to send you notifications of changes of their terms. Always remember that the original agreement between you and your credit card company can change anytime. The law only requires the issuer to send you a 15 day notice before the change kick in. You can always save money by protecting yourself, if you keep up with the changes in the terms. Apart from secure credit card, you can get a credit from any established creditor, and after the credit is paid off completely, you can ask the creditor to write a letter of recommendation for you and send a copy to the credit reporting agencies. This is because many agencies will include letters of recommendations in their official credit reports. You can also give this letter of recommendation to a potential lender when you apply for a loan. You can also get a personal loan or line of credit from a bank or financial institution and make your payments on time. If you do, they will report your credit and payments history to credit bureaus.

Debit cards And ATM Bank cards

Debit cards are the opposite of credit cards. With debit cards, your purchase is directly deducted from your bank account. The charge only goes through when you have the money in your account. This kind of account eliminates the possibility of you going over your limit and mounting up interest charges. The Bank you use, and many other financial institutions, offers this service, but they do not get the hype, like the credit card services get. This is because these companies can make more money off you by watching you run your credit bills up. Do not forget that ATM cards can also be used as debit cards. You should ask your bank when opening an account or the bank you are using if there is any different between their debit card and ATM card. Remember that some bank may charge a fee for using the debit or ATM card, especially when you use the card at ATM's that is not own by your bank.

What most creditors look for in your credit report?

1. **Missed payments by you:** How often you miss payments? How long ago? They check your outstanding credit cards payments

2. **Time:** The time of your credit. For example, if you have been holding a credit card for twenty years and you have been paying on time, but late for the past five years, it is not that important.

3. **Total debt:** How much debt do you have today? And how much debt are you going to have tomorrow? If you keep on opening credit card accounts, there is a greater risk you could be in greater debt.

These are some reasons you need to check your credit

◊   To make sure mistakes on your credit are not going to hurt your credit.

◊   To keep track of your payment history.

◊   To protect you against potential identity theft

◊   To help you try to keep your credit inquiries to a minimum.

◊   To stay on top of your credit without hurting your credit score.

FICO—Fair Isaac and Company

This Company is a name everyone should be familiar with before applying for credit of any kind—be it credit card, car loan, mortgages etc. This company is located in San Rafael, California and it created the widely used computer-scoring model that assigns people their scores, based on information they have in their credit files. The numbers they assign range from 300 to 850. 300 is the lowest, while 850 is the highest. In this case, the higher the score, the lower the risk, therefore the lower the interest rate you might have to pay for a home, a car or auto loan. The score you get from credit bureaus and e-loans are similar but not the same. You can easily get your FICO score for $12.95 from three websites—Myfico.com—or equifax.com and transunioncs.com.

Experian sells their scores based on its own model to consumers for $14.95. Knowing your credit score is very important, especially if you are in the habit of paying bills late, maybe carrying a stack of credit cards, or just making minimum payments.

> The number one enemy of personal finance is procrastination.
>
> —Dave Chilton, The wealthy Barber

What can make or kill your credit

If you make a thirty-day-late payment a month ago, it will count against you more than a ninety-day-late payment you made five years ago. If you have a small balance without missing a payment, it is better than having no credit balance at all. In other words, your track record as to how you have been paying your bills does matters. Any lender would want to know whether you have paid your credit cards bills on time. Late payments do not automatically kill your credit score. The overall picture of your credit history can outweigh one or two instances of late credit card payments. You should know that having no late payments in your credit history report does not mean you will get a perfect score.

What you really need to do is pay your bills on time, keep your credit card balances as low as possible, and then you can apply for new credit cards. If these are carefully followed, it will keep your credit score in good shape. You should know that having credit accounts and owing money on them does not mean you are a high-risk borrower. On the other hand, owing a great deal of money on many accounts can indicate that you are overextended and more likely to make some payments late or not make some payments at all. The part of the scoring science you need to understand is determining how much is too much for a given credit profile. Some financial counselors will advise that you should not use more than 50 percent of your limits, especially if you have many credit cards. Many researches have shown that opening several credit accounts in a very short period represent greater risk. Too many inquiries to the credit report agencies also represent a risk. These are request by lenders for a copy of your credit report. Opening credit accounts that you do not use or intend to use, like a department store card, just to get the 10 percent discount can also affect your credit score.

Trying to make a major purchase?

Check out your credit score, from myfico.com or the other two credit reporting agencies excluding experian, check out the interest rate. You can do this on bankrates.com or banx.com. Checking it out will really give you an insight on the journey you are about to take. You will know the interest rates most lenders are charging and this will really let you know where you stand. This is because if you have bad credit, most lenders will charge you higher interest rate.

The higher your credit score numbers, the better you look to lenders.

Credit Card bills and late fees

If you have trouble paying your credit card bills, you need to contact your creditors. Anytime you fail to make payments, there will be penalty fees added to the amount that you owe. These penalty fees can really jack up the amount that you owe. You should always let your creditors know your situation and ask them for reduction in your monthly payments. Most creditors, after they wait for your payments for about six months and did not receive any, they usually charge off or write off the credit card debt for tax purpose.

And they will usually continue to bug you through in-house or outside collection agency. When they turn your account to a collection agency, you should negotiate a deal with the collection agency. This is because most collection agencies, will accept a partial payment to settle the account and then report your "charge-off" to credit bureaus as a "settled charge-off." If you did not settle with the collection agency, they might sue you.

You should always make sure you look at the due dates on your bills, especially the credit card bills. Some of the credit cards companies charge up to $50 as late fee and some can even go higher. You can call the creditor if you might be late making your payment and see if they can waive the late fee and this practice is applicable to most loans, car loans, mortgages and credit card loans. If you have problems paying your bills, it is important for you to call your creditors and let them know that you are having some financial difficulties. In most cases, your creditor is always willing to work with you.

Credit Cards value

Most people start to establish their credit worthiness through credit card or cards that they acquire. This could be gas card, departmental store card, bank card etc. Since most people start from here, there are very high interest rates charges on credit cards and it is a big business because of the interest rate that is charged. Every month, the credit card company asked the holder for a minimum payment. This required payment is calculated based on the new loan balance. Just as the balance on the credit card goes down, the minimum required payment comes down as well. This kind of arrangement has a secret catch to it. The interest that you pay for each payment remain large and the part of the total amount from your payment goes to the principal—which is actually the amount you owe—remain small, this makes the loan to go on and on for years. This is why it takes years to payoff a credit card if you are just making the minimum required payment on your credit card.

You should not only watch out for the low interest rate on the credit card, you should also watch out for the minimum payment required by the creditor. This is because if the interest rate is low and the required minimum payment is low, it will still take you years to pay off, sometimes it can take more years than a card with high interest rate that require higher minimum payment.

Credit card is a good way to established or re-establish your credit, but it is not a good credit, especially if you are in financial hardship and you cannot make the payments. You can make the minimum payments for years. One of the reasons why many people own many credit cards is because they did not really know much about credit cards and sometime they do not have good financial plans. An average consumer with six or more credit card is not a sound financial plan. According to Consumer Federation of America, people with incomes between $10,000 and $100,000 who say they have a written financial plan report twice much money in savings and investment as people without a plan. You will succeed more if you have a plan for paying off your credit card debts, especially paying at the end of the month what you spent.

The best way to pay off your credit cards debt is to first and foremost look at the interest rates on those credit cards. For example, if you have 6 credit cards with interest rates ranging from 1% to 6%, you should try talking to the creditors, starting from the one with the highest interest rate to see if they can reduce the interest rate. Secondly, you should see if the card with the lowest interest rate can allow you to transfer or consolidate all other credit cards into the account you have with them. And if all these fail, you should try as much as possible to pay off the one with the highest interest rate first and then move on to the next one with the higher interest rate. This is simply laddering your payment plan. If you are going to consolidate, make sure that you use a loan with lower interest rate to pay off the debt with a higher interest rate. When you call your creditors, always try to negotiate for a lower interest rate on your credit card, if you don't, you are not helping yourself toward quick payoff of the credit card debt.

You should always keep in mind that credit cards are loans, if you cannot pay back the loan and you successfully negotiate with your creditor for reduced pay back, maybe because you are trying to avoid bankruptcy, you will be taxed on it by IRS. This is because the IRS considers "forgiveness of a loan" a taxable activity. Uncle Sam may want to make his share of the discount as if it were income to you. The credit company will actually seek your approval on the tax form (1099).

The real truth behind Credit cards

America society and many societies in civilized world today place a lot of on credit cards; some hotels will not accept reservations from a potential guest without a credit card. Some restaurants do the same. Some car rentals and internet stores only accept credit cards. This has saved some of the e-commerce website a lot of money because they don't have to have someone stay by the phone twenty four seven. Department stores, gas stations, local drug stores, retail outlets, home shopping network all offer and accept credit cards these days. You can make many powerful and expensive purchases right from your home computer, through the television with your credit cards. Those plastics are so powerful that they can give you a tremendous respect or disgrace when turned down. Due to the plastic cards, many people who otherwise would not have had a very high purchasing power now do. These cards are very convenient, because they are light and can prevent you from carrying cash around. These days some of the credit cards have picture of the owner in front of them to prevent theft. You can get gifts and freebies these days just for using your credit cards. You can get gift certificates, discount for car rentals and hotel.

Trouble with Credit cards

You have to use and handle credit cards responsibly and wisely. This is because many people in this so call civilized world end up spending the money they don't have in the name of credit cards. As we all know, credit card is about you spending now and paying later. "The individual who, by his or her nature, seeks instant gratification is more likely to run into credit card debt than the person who plans ahead." You should have rules that guide your spending habits. Some people employ rules that let them use credit cards for major expenses and in emergencies. You should always keep an eye on your checking account, since you pay for your credit cards from this account. It is not good money management if a $25 check did not clear and the bank charge you $30, sometimes the credit company may charge you as well.

Expensive truth about credit cards: Take for example, you owe $10,000 on one of your credit cards, and the interest rate is 19%, then your monthly minimum payment is calculated as 2% of your outstanding balance. Under this example, if you don't switch your $10,000 debt to a lower interest loan, and you choose to only send in the required minimum payments, by the time you've paid it off about 50 years from now, you would have paid back more than three times what you owed. This will be about $33,447. The card company will have received $23,447 in interest alone. In other words, every $50 purchase will cost you $167. This is why it is very hard for borrowers to get rich and people who are debt free are getting richer. Think twice before you use that card next time to buy groceries.

The status of limitation: The credit cards companies have about four years in most states to come after you for their money when you refuse to pay and once the status is passed the creditor cannot take you to court. If you choice to pay it off after the status of limitation, make a deal with the credit card company or collection agency to pay a portion for a write off and make sure they did not slap you with a 1099 (tax form).

Lawsuit: When a collection agency or a law firm sues you for non-payment, you should respond to the lawsuit. Do not just ignore it. If you fail to respond in writing, this depends on your state of residence, the lawyer or the agency can have the court enter a default judgment against you. This default judgment can lead to some of your wages been garnished or even seizure of your bank account or even a lien place against your property. You should know that you have right here after the default judgment has been granted in your absent. You may have a good excuse for not responding to their letters or not showing up in court maybe you were ill, or traveled out of town or did not even receive the summons from the lawyer or from the court. It could be that your identity was stolen and your card was reported missing. This can be a very good defense. You should write to the court clerk or the judge and ask for the judgment to be **set aside.** Explain why you were not in court. You can dispute any of this kind of judgment within 30 days. At this point, if your excuse is legitimate, the judgment can be dropped or you will be given a new court dates for you to come and defend yourself. You are entitled to a due process.

Note: You should find out if the judgment was obtained from a small claim court. Most small claim court cases are litigations that are $5,000 and below. If a judgment was obtained from a small claim court, it may not be effective if you re-locate to another state.

How the credit card Industry works

You should know how this industry works before holding on to those credit cards. This will help you to be responsible with the usage. The credit card issuers, be it a bank, a store, or some institution are giving you a loan to buy goods and services and this loan has limit on it, like any other loan. The limit means the maximum amount they can extend to you. They will send you a monthly bill or statement and in it, you will see your activities. If you pay the bill on time or if you pay it in full, you will not incur other charges. Apart from the high interest rate, you will be charged if you did not pay in full. In most cases, they will charge you certain amount when you charge above the limit.

Some companies also charge annual fees. They may promise you some other services, but you will still pay a fee for the convenience of spending without using cash—This is also applicable if you use your debit card as credit card. Make sure you always check all these out before using the credit card.

Choosing a credit card

Which is best for you—Visa or MasterCard, in light of how you use bank cards? The following credit-card rating services may help you answer that question. Bank rate.com located in North Palm Beach., Fl, Surveys the nation's banks weekly and compiles its findings in its Best Credit Card List. When ordering, select a list based on whether you carry a credit-card balance or pay your bill in full each month. The cost of this service is $10. Call 1-800-327-7717, extension 407, for the list of your choice or visit Bankrate.com.

You choose your credit as you would when making any other major purchases. This is also important, because the requirements by the issuer vary. First you should take a look at the payment features, which include looking at all the other discounts they may offer you.

What to look for:

1. **Interest rate:** First make sure that the low interest rate does not only apply to your transfer balance, just for the sake of it. You should read the fine print when applying for a credit card. For comprehensive lists of low-interest-rate credit cards check out: www.consumer-action.org or card-trak.com

2. **How they calculate the interest rate**
    Most companies usually figure out the interest using the average daily balance, adjusted balance or previous balance. Look out for plans that are proposing two cycle balances. This is because this method charges interests that have already accrued.

3   **Charged fee:** We know that almost all credit cards charges one form of fee or the other. Look out for these fees. It could be late fee, over-the-limit fee, annual fee, transaction fee and so on. Sometimes it could even be inactivity fee—which they charge you if you did not use the card for a specified period of time. Sometimes they may charge you if you accept a credit limit increase. They can charge you penalty fee if you pay off your balance or close your account. You need to know all of these before you apply for the credit card.

4   **Grace Period:** Some credit cards companies look out for grace period to see if you pay off the balance, for example, some may expect you to pay your account in full each month. If they did not receive the payment by certain date, they will impose a finance charge or some fee.

5   **Fixed or variable rate:** You should bear in mind that fixed interest rate on your credit card sometimes increase. Find out if they are permanent or if they are only offered during the introductory period. You should read the fine print before signing it.

Acquiring a credit card

1.   **Keep one bank card** and one department store card. Cut the other cards up. Multiple cards only encourage unnecessary spending.

2.   **Avoid 'upscale' cards—gold, silver, platinum etc:** An American Express green card costs $55 a year, the gold card $75, and the platinum $350 a year. Their value begins and ends with snob appeal. A higher line of credit for a higher fee at credit-card interest rates is no bargain.

3.   **Shop for bank cards:** All Master Cards and Visa are the same regarding usage. What you pay for them is not. Some banks charge no annual fee, others up to $35. Some charge less than 8-percent interest, others up to 18 percent. The highest annual percentage rate (APR) is often charged by major bank-card advertisers; you bear the cost of those ads in user fees.

4.   **If you belong to a credit union, apply for a member's credit card:** Credit union terms are usually more favorable than a bank's terms and rates

5.   **Charge only what you can afford to pay back in full every month:** This way you avoid finance charges that you will pay altogether.

6.   **Avoid using department-store cards for purchases like TVs or furniture:** You can often borrow the money for these purchases from your bank or credit union at lower rates. Better still, save in advance and pay cash. You may even get a lower price that way.

7.   **Compare monthly finance charges on cards you choose to keep:** For example, J.C. Penney and Montgomery Ward both have their own credit cards, but also accept Visa and MasterCard. You may be paying a lower interest rate on your bank card than on the store card.

The three credit bureaus

Equifax
To order a report: 1-800-685-1111
or write: P.O. Box 740241, Atlanta, GA 30374-0241
To report fraud: 1-800-525-6285
and write: P.O. Box 740241, Atlanta, GA 30374-0241
www.equifax.com

Experian
To order a report: 1-888-EXPERIAN (397-3742)
or write: P.O. Box 2104, Allen, TX 75013
To report fraud: 1-888-EXPERIAN (397-3742)
and write: P.O. Box 9532, Allen, TX 75013
www.experian.com

TransUnion
To order a report: 800-916-8800
or write: P.O. Box 1000, Chester, PA 19022
To report fraud: 1-800-680-7289
and write: Fraud Victim Assistance Division, P.O. Box 6790, Fullerton, CA 92634
www.transunion.com

All these credit cards are tracked by the "big three" credit bureaus. These credit bureaus do not write your credit report. They only take information from the companies you deal with, like your credit card companies and collection agencies. They then sell this information that they gather to potential credit grantors. The credit bureaus build a report on your buying and paying habits and these reports are use when you apply for credit.

Credit card Approval or Denial Process

When you apply for a credit card, your application goes to a processing center clerk where the clerk will enter your personal information into a computer. If you fill out the credit card application over the internet for instant credit approval or denial, you bypass the clerk. If you meet the basic requirement like minimum income, the computer will dial credit bureau to get your credit report information. The computer will evaluate how much of a risk you are to the lender. This is done by them using their credit scoring system. The goal of this system is to compare the things people who pay their bills on time have in common with each other, and what things those who don't pay their bills on time have in common. It will use all these to predict whether the potential customer will pay on time or not.

These are some of the factors they might be looking for:

- How many credit cards you may have
- What are the other types of loans you may have
- How many times you have been late making payments
- How much you owe on all your bills and maybe more.

If you get a passing score after the evaluation, you will get an approval and a credit card from the lender. If you did not get a passing score, you will get a denial and then a rejection letter from the lender. This may be generated automatically by the computer. Some of the lenders out there may have a different way of assigning points to their potential credit card customers.

Your rights if you are denied credit

- You have the right to know the name and address of the agency that prepared the report that was used to deny you credit. If you want to get the information, it is necessary for you to make the request in writing to any creditor that has refused credit.
- If you are refused credit, you have the right to review your file with the reporting agency for free. You can also obtain a copy of the case history file. Your request must be made within thirty days of notification of credit refusal.
- The negative information cannot be reported beyond seven years, with the exception of a bankruptcy, which can be reported for ten years.

Take charge of your credit card debt

You should always read the fine print before signing for a credit card. Do not accept the card without first understanding the terms and conditions. Since credit cards are many out there, it is very necessary to find out which one really fit your needs. The most popular credit cards today are visa and MasterCard. All these credit cards only give you a line of credit. They expect you to pay back for the loan, but they will charge you interest and other charges. American Express card works like a charge card, unlike a line of credit. American Express essentially pays the bill for you. As such, the cardholder is not allowed to pay in increments. The balance must be paid in full for whatever was charged at the end of the 30-day cycle. They make money on fees they charge to merchants and the yearly fees they charge to cardholders. However, American Express also offers the Optima card, which allows you to make monthly payments in the same manner as visa and MasterCard.

Look at the privileges that a card offers, like frequent flier mileage, savings on long-distance calls, store discounts etc. You should keep in mind that these "extras" don't have fees or other requirements attached. You should find out what the company can do for you as their cardholder. There are companies out there that can help you do practically anything and in anyplace in the world. Some of the companies may fail to tell you that you have to sign up for the special services in advance or charge up to a certain amount on the card. Some of these rewards are offered only on cards such as gold cards or platinum cards.

Do not fall for many companies out there that promise to send you a free credit card; this will lead to too many credit cards that you might not be able to pay for. It is to your best interest to stick with a few credit cards that you know you will actually use and can afford to pay for in full at the end of the month. You should not apply for a credit card every time you receive an application in your mail. If you apply, it will be marked down on your credit rating. This is also true because applying for many cards can make a lender nervous; they see that you run up a large amount of debt. They will refuse to extend you credit if they think you already owe several other credit cards.

Creditors' New ways to get you

- **Reporting your past debt as new debt:** Some collection agencies sometimes try as much as they can to pressure borrowers to repay their debt. They pick debt that are about to be dropped from the borrowers' credit report, and this is against the Fair Credit Reporting Act's which is seven year statute of limitations. They report it as new debt, with a new date. This debt could remain on the credit report for another seven years. This is a scheme and it is illegal. It happens to many people everyday. You should always check your credit at list ones a year.

- **Sudden Changes on an account:** Some creditors may change the rules in the middle of the game. They will change their junk fees on you without you knowing it. For example you may find out in your statement that the grace period—the time you must pay the bill before interest charges and late fees kick in has been narrowed from 30 days to 20 days. You should always check your bill very well.

- **Carry over of old debt:** Most of the credit cards companies work together to make sure the debt does not go unpaid. One company can forego your debt, and when you apply to get a card from a different company, they will bring back the old debt. Take for example if Chase Manhattan Bank forgave your credit card debt a couple of years ago, you can apply for a capitalOne card and the debt is included. Watch and read the blue print carefully before you sign it.

- **The 0% rates:** The 0% rate is not really 0% rate. Most credit cards companies give this rate to their best customers. You typically will pay 3% as balance transfer fee and 0% rate will apply only to certain parts of your balance.

- **Bank credit card interest rates:** Many credit-card lenders have instituted in their profits, a minimum interest rates. Check the fine print to be sure about your cards, because the banks are not happy when interest rate drops.

- **Time you made your payment:** Some companies have to receive your payment within a certain time, for example by noon. If they received it in their mail room after 12 noon, they will charge you late fee. The only way you can bit this is to pay your credit card bill as soon as you receive it.

Credit Insurance: debt-suspension, debt-cancellation and credit insurance fee has gone up considerably. These are contracts marketed to people who are worried about paying their bills if they die, become disables or if they lose their jobs. Contracts are now overpriced in many cases. If you need this kind of insurance you should seriously shop around for low premiums.

The right way to cancel your credit card

Know if the interest rate will rise

You need to find out if the interest rate is going to be jacked up before you cancel your credit card. Most companies will change the interest rate as soon as you cancel your account—for example from 19.99% to 39.99%. Call the company first. Most of them will not tell you.

Let the issuer know by phone

The credit cards issuer's customer-service number will be printed on the back of your credit card, on the monthly statement, or both. Call that number, confirm that your balance is zero, and notify the customer-service representative that you're canceling the card. If you truly intend to cancel the card, hold firm if the rep tries to talk you out of it by promising lower rates or fees.

Send a letter as a follow up

Send a short letter to the card issuer. If you can get a name so you can send it directly to the name that is better. The letter should say that you're closing your account and that you want your credit record to reflect the fact that you requested that the account be closed. Provide your name, address and account number. Send the letter by certified mail or return receipt requested. That way you can prove that the card issuer received your letter, Brannan says. Then, wait a month." "You can allow as much as 30 days for the closing of your account," Brannan says. "Then get a copy of your credit report and make sure it says 'Closed at customer's request' and that (the account) actually has been taken off your credit report."

Check on your credit report

Don't let your credit report to say the account was "closed by creditor," because that reflects negatively on you. If the card issuer mistakenly reported that the issuer, not you, closed the account, you'll have to return to the beginning. Call the customer-service department to report the mistake, follow up with a letter sent by certified mail (include a copy of the letter you wrote requesting that the account be closed), and check your credit report again.

"Remember that a credit report is your credit history," Brannan says. "The information is submitted by lenders, but it's your individual responsibility to make sure it's correct."

Understand that, it's not the credit bureau's responsibility to make sure that your credit report is correct. Credit bureaus report what creditors tell them. So if your credit report is inaccurate, don't ask the credit bureau to fix it. Ask the creditors to correct inaccuracies and update the credit bureaus. Experts recommend that you check your credit report annually to spot inaccuracies and detect identity-theft problems. Check your credit report before buying a house or car so you can correct any problems before applying for a loan.

The benefits of some credit cards

Credit cards like "Gold/platinum/titanium cards offer more benefits (accrue frequent flier mileage faster, rental insurance, purchase protection) than normal cards but also have higher annual membership fees. Cash back cards (Discover, US west MasterCard) offer money back based on the level of purchases. Hotel cards (Caesar's Gold MasterCard, Marriott First Card) offer points towards discounts on dining, entertainment, merchandise, and hotel stays."

You really have to shop around to find out what type of discount the credit offers and the one that fit your needs. You can get what may be tailored toward your lifestyle. For example, you may be a frequent flier, you may be going on frequent vacations, seek out hotels and car rental deals. You may be interested in just low interest rates. You need to really try and shop around.

Credit cards make goods and services easily accessible to consumers today than ever before. Many people are not responsible spenders, and these people need to take some responsibilities for their actions. You should know what you can afford and what you cannot afford before you buy, because the bill is going to come at the end of the month. If you ask your neighbor to lend you $10 anytime you are about to step out of the house, you will know that it is adding up anytime you come back home. You will know what you are up against whenever you come back. But with credit cards, you easily forget where your charge comes from because you do not see the lender.

How to build a good credit

- **Have a checking and savings accounts:** This kind of accounts is very important, because lenders will like to know that you have an easier way to pay your bills. Any one can do this, because bank account teaches you how to manage your money.

- **Get your credit report ones or twice a year:** You use your credit report to know how you are viewed by lenders on regular basis. In case you don't know what suppose to be in your report, try and order one and you will see it. Before you even look at other things in it, make sure the name and social security number in it is yours.

- **Fix the omissions and errors:** When you get your credit report, fix whatever is not accurate, by first of all filing out the complained and dispute form that will come with it. Try to correct the negative information, like late payments, delinquencies, liens, and judgments against you. But bankruptcies stay for 7 to 10 years in your file.

- **Include positive information in your credit report:** The more positive information you have there the more lenders will value your credit worthiness. Your job and resident should also appear stable; this is apart from paying your bills on time.
    - o Is your employer and job title in the report? If you have had a job for less than two years, your previous employer and job title will be listed as well.

o   Make sure your social security is correct and listed. This is how most lenders know who you are.

o   What about your telephone number? Is it listed and is it correct? Many lenders cannot give you credit if they cannot call you.

o   What about your payment history? Are they all included in your report? You can ask any of your creditors that are not listed to report your good credit to credit bureaus.

Credit Collectors

Consumer credit collection act control all persons who regularly collect debts. These people could be attorneys, professional collection agencies, and some office personnel's. Do not forget the word here is "regularly" If they collect debt on an irregular basis, then they are not affected. For example, if your doctor's office calls you for the debt you owe, which they don't do regularly, they are not covered by the act. A collector can contact you between 8:00am and 6:00pm. They cannot contact you at an inconvenient or unusual time, such as late evening or early in the morning. A collector cannot contact you at work, especially if you have told them not to do so. A collector may not call other people more than once to find out about your current address, and may not discuss your debt with other people. If you have a lawyer, they should contact your attorney. You can stop collector's harassment by writing them and telling them not to contact you again. The worse case scenario is a legal action by the creditor. If you don't owe the debt they have contacted you in writing about, you should write them within 30 days to dispute their allegations.

A collector, who violates the law, can be sued by you. The collection agency can pay you if you win the sum of $500,000 or 1 percent of the agency's net worth, whichever is lower. You should report any violation of the consumer credit collection act to the state attorney general's office or Federal trade commission in Washington D.C.

No debtors prison in America. You should not be afraid that you will go to jail if you cannot pay your bills. Look at the worse case scenario. The creditor will not lock you up. All they can do is get a judgment from the court and go after your assets. This has to do with credit cards debt, but we all know if it is something they can take back, they will—like a car or a house. If collection agencies won't leave you alone when you cannot pay the credit card debt, here is a "Drop dead letter" you can send to them.

"Drop dead letter"

Your Address

Date

Ref Acct #

Dear Executive;

Your Company contacted me regarding a debt you claim I owe.

I hereby instruct you not to contact me again regarding this allege debt.

Under the fair debt collection practices Act, a federal law, you may not contact me again once I have asked you not to contact me again.

Sincerely,
Sign your name

Errors on your credit report

You may be listed with two or three of the "big three" credit bureaus—Equifax, experian and transunion. You should always check all three at least ones a year. You can request for free report ones a year and within thirty days after you have been turned down for a credit. You can call them or simply go to their website and fill out a form. Some merchants incorrectly report purchases or sometimes fail to report that you have paid off your delinquent bill. You have to prove that it is really an error, by filling out a dispute form for them to investigate and take it out of your credit report. Sometimes they may mistakenly put someone else information in your credit report. Sometimes, getting errors corrected is a long process. First you can start out by filling out the accompanying form that they send to you with your credit report. Although errors are common, but this kind of errors if not corrected can affect your life. If after you are polite and patient, they cannot correct the error, you need to call the office of the attorney general of your state or the Federal trade commission in Washington DC.

Stolen or lost credit cards

You should copy or write down the toll-free number of the issuer of your credit card with you in case your credit card is lost or stolen. You should report it quickly ones it is stolen or lost, so that the issuer can cancel the card. This will help you not to be billed for subsequent charges to your card. You should call immediately because in most cases, if the card has already been used, you may be liable for a small amount of the used amount. Review your credit card bill immediately and carefully anytime you receive one, since it is important to the company know of any charges that obviously do not belong to you. Some people usually discover that their credit card is stolen or lost when they discover erroneous charges on their credit card bill. "An alert credit card company will call you or even request identification at the point of purchase if the card is used for a series of transactions in a short period of time."

Fixing identity theft problem

- Contact or send a certify letter denying the debt charges to all the collections agencies that contacted you. Make sure you keep a copy for your record.

- Give then at least 21 days to respond to your letter.

- If you did not hear from them, send a second letter and give them about 14 days to respond—make sure you keep a copy for your record.

- If you still can't get it resolved, then start talking to an attorney and inform the agency through your attorney that you will sue them for violating the fair credit collection act.

Credit rating

Our credit rating, as we all know, follows us throughout our lives. It helps us to make a major purchase at a lower interest rate if our credit is good and it can hurt us if our credit is bad. We need a good credit to prove that we are credit worthy in the eyes of our lenders. Apart from the fact that people move from job to job these days, lenders still like to see that you have stayed at a job for a long period of time. They like to see that you pay your bills on time. They also like to know about your assets, earnings and investments. When a lender is trying to determine if you are a good bet, they check out all the facts about your job, earning, assets, investment and payment history. Although some credit cards companies make it so easy to get their credit cards because they want people to carry their cards, but these cards are usually not good offers if you read their fine prints carefully. Remember, they are sellers and they have the right to solicit for customers, so don't fall a prey next time you receive pr-approval letter in the mail.

Balance Transfer that are Tricky

◊ **Tease-rates:** Some credit cards companies offer great introductory rates on balance transfer. Sometimes, these rates last nine months to five years. You have to really read the fine print and continue to follow what the company is doing regarding your account; this is because it is easy for them to jack up the price. It could be either because you pay late or you went over the limit, before you know it they will jack up the rate from say 2.99% to 19.99% interest rate.

◊ **Making new purchases with the new card:** Some of these cards will not charge interest for six months on new purchases—cards like American Express Blue card is 0% interest rate for the first six months. Some of them hold the interest steady at low rate until you pay off your transfer balance according to the stipulated contract. Read the blue print very well before you transfer your credit balance from an old card to a new card.

◊ **Be cautious:** You should be careful, because they might sound like good deals, but they carry a lot of hidden penalties. Some of these companies charge transfer fee, which they will not tell you.

◊ **Don't stop paying for the old card:** You should continue to make at least minimum payments on the old card until you are 100% sure the transfer is complete.

◊ **All the interest rates are not applicable in all cases:** You should read the teeny, tiny print near the end of the credit application offer. The offer might say 1.9% interest rate on balance transfers, but you may only qualify for 10.99% interest rate.

◊ **Get your worth from the new card:** After you get the new credit card and get the low interest rate, you will have a breathing space and be able to pay the credit card and save some money for a raining day.

How to increase your credit Score

The score system is a three digit system and 11% of the surveyed population scored above 800; while 29% scored between 750 and 799 and the sores of this system range from 300 to 850. Lenders use this scoring system to evaluate your creditworthiness.

1. **Pay bills on time:** Payment history carries a lot of weight when lenders are evaluating your credit worthiness. The latest payments carry more weight than the late payments you made five years ago. If you want to have a good

credit score, pay your bills on time. The next in line is delinquent payment. You can avoid late payment if you automate your bill payment with different software's out there like quickens, MSN Money, online bill pay etc.

2. **Pay it down before you apply for loan:** If you will like to apply for a home mortgage or a car loan, start paying down your bills about a year in advance before you apply.

3. **Start charging less:** If you start charging way below the credit limit, it will make you look good to the lender. If you always max your credit cards, it look risky.

4. **Do not close accounts:** If you have paid off your credit card account, you should not close that account, because if you close it, it will not show up in your credit report and it will make you look to lenders as not credit worthy.

5. **Have few credit cards:** The next time you get a new credit card offer in the mail, you should not accept, especially if you already have two or more credit cards. Even if a department store clerk offer you a 10% discount if you sign up for their card. They have the right to make solicitation for your business and you have the right to turn them down.

6. **Do not go into bankruptcy:** Bankruptcy is not good in your credit report. It is worst than loans defaults, or delinquencies and collections. Bankruptcy can reduce your credit score with up to 200 points off.

7. **Have credit below your worth:** make sure you don't over strength your credit, because if you have too much debt, your debt ratio will prevent lenders from giving you more credit.

8. **Get credit counseling:** If you find your self deep in debt, use credit counseling service. Make sure the services you are using are working for you not for the creditors.

Credit Cards Security Tips

1. **Don't lose your card:** Always keep eye on your card, don't leave the store without your card.

2. **Card receipt should be shredded or burned:** Don't just keep your receipt lying around in the office or at home.

3. **Beware of people behind you with cell phones:** Some people can use their camera phone to snap picture of your card or receipt at the store.

4. **No solicitors should be given your number:** This can be telemarketers, magazine subscriptions or vacation purchases by phone.

5. **Check your charges:** Every now and then check your statement to make sure you recognize all the charges and the merchants.

6. **Report unexpected charges:** If you find charges that you did not make, report them immediately to your creditors.

7. **Tell your creditors not to send you checks:** Call your creditors and let them know that you don't need such checks.

8. **Always know when your statements arrive:** If your statements do not arrive on your expected dates, check with your creditors. Maybe they are stolen.

9. **Sometimes make copies of your cards:** Keep the copies of the front and back in a secure place other than your wallet.

10. **Do not carry many cards:** This can help you in case your wallet is stolen, the thief will not do too much damage to you.

11. **Don't fall for e-mail links:** Some credit card thieves can send you email with a link to make sure your card is active, asking you to enter your card number when you click on the link that they are your issuer. The link will actually take you to the criminal's website without you knowing.

12. **Have a locked mailed box if possible:** This can prevent someone from pretending to be dropping something off for you in your mailbox, where as they are stealing your mails.

MORTGAGES AND CAR LOANS FACTS

No man's credit is ever as good as his money

—Edgar Watson Howe

The Most common long term expense today

I will say housing loan is the most common expense because most people cannot afford to buy house cash or free and clear. This long term expense is unavoidable. It is very significant and we spend at least 29 percent of our disposable income on housing. As such, saving money on your mortgage can make a great difference in your financial picture. Save money on your mortgage. Apart from getting a good deal, the right time and location, one of the best ways to save on your mortgage is to make additional payments toward your principal every month. Banks and mortgage companies don't really like this because you are preventing them from making the kind of profit they expect to make. If you pay more, it will enable you to easily pay it off free and clear, so that you only worry about the taxes repairs and insurance. Some savings and loan companies and Banks offer mortgage payment acceleration program to help you pay off your mortgage on time. Some Banks may call it equity enhancement program or some other kind of name. In most cases, they will make you pay bi-weekly by withdrawing the money directly from your checking account. They usually charge some money to set up this kind of mortgage payment. This is really a rip off by the bank, because I think it is not suppose to cost the customer. In any case, you can do the same by yourself. Make sure you ask your mortgage or finance company if there is penalty for prepay before you prepay.

For example: "You borrowed $100,000 for a home at 9% interest rate for 30 years. Your monthly payments would be $804.62 per month in principal and interest. In the thirty years, you will pay $289,663 and $189,663 will be the interest. You could 'prepay' the loan and reduce its life to twenty-five years by

$34.58 more in principal each month. You could reduce your total interest by $37,903 and pay it off five years earlier."

Make your monthly payment shrink

"With Mortgages, car, and student loans, as well as most other debts, when you sign it, you receive a set minimum payment and term. For example, on a $100,000 and a 30 year mortgage at a 7%, your principal and interest amount would equal $665.31 per month (not including taxes and insurance). Credit cards don't work the same way. Each month, the required payment is calculated based on the new loan balance. As the balance goes down, the required payment goes down as well."

Most people usually choose 30 years mortgage, but if you can afford the 15 years mortgage, you should go for it because it is better. Although "prepay" works better on a 30 years mortgage than on a 15 years mortgage. Many financial advisers are always working for the interest of the banks and financial institutions that is why they will advise you not to pay off your mortgage. Some of them use the tax deductions as their reasons, but you should know that you are only giving Uncle Sam an interest free loan and wait until the end of the year to see what you can get back. If you are in a 30% tax bracket, you luckily can only get back 3 cents on every dollar loan you gave to Uncle Sam as interest on your mortgage.

What about the peace of mind of you knowing that you don't have to worry about the roof over your head. You truly own a house free and clear. This is supposed to be when you OWN the house rather than the popular banking and financial institutions definition of ownership which is really OWE on the house. One of the best financial gift you can give to your children and love ones in your retirement age is not to financially take care of you. And having a house paid for, especially before you retire is one way to do it and it will prolong your life, because you will worry less about the roof over your head.

What Lenders may and may not ask you by Law.

Lenders may ask:

◊   To know your permanent residency or immigration status.

◊   To know the number of dependents and dependent-related financial obligations.

◊   To know your marital status if you are applying for a joint account or one secured by property, or if you live in a community property state.

◊   About your spouse if any of the following apply: You live in a community property state; the spouse is a co-applicant; the spouse will share use of the account; you rely on your spouse's income; you rely on child support or alimony from a former spouse.

◊   If you pay alimony, child support or separate maintenance payments.

◊   For the names under which you have previously received credit.

Lenders may not:

◊   Ask for your sex, race, color, religion or national origin.

◊   Ask about your plans for raising or having children in the future.

◊   Ask whether you are married or your marital status when you apply for a separate, unsecured account, unless you live in a community property state such as Arizona, California, Idaho, Louisiana, Nevada, New Mexico, Texas and Washington.

◊   Ask whether you are receiving alimony, child support or separate maintenance payments UNLESS you will rely on that income to pay back credit. A lender must explain that the income from these sources need not be revealed unless the applicant wishes to rely on it to establish creditworthiness.

◊   Give you a discount or refuse to consider your income because it comes from part-time work, pension, annuity or retirement benefits.

◊   Give you or your spouse a discount income because of your sex or marital status. For example, a creditor cannot count a man's salary at 100% and a woman's at 75%.

◊   Make the assumption that a woman will stop working to raise children.

◊   Ask you to voluntarily disclose your sex, race and national origin if you're applying for a real estate loan.

Refinancing your mortgage

If you are considering refinancing, checkout the interest rates that the market is presently offering at bankrate.com. Check out your credit report. FICO, the credit scoring system most lenders use. Unfortunately, FICO does not punish you if you do mortgage shopping in a condensed time. "All credit inquiries made within 14 days are lumped together as one, and your score doesn't reflect any inquiries made within the last 30 days."

When interest rate is low, many people want to refinance and many lenders are very busy.

Make a choice: Decide ahead of time what kind of loan you want.

◊   Fixed-rate loan—either 15, 20, 25, or 30 years

◊   ARM—adjustable rate Mortgage loan

◊   Hybrid—It remain fixed for some years before becoming adjustable

How to speed up the process

Paperwork: You can choice "low-doc" or "no-doc" loan to reduce the paperwork that the lender will process. Some of these less documentation loans might charge more or less interest. One other thing you should know about the fast-track loan is that they may eliminate some steps like income and asset verification if you have good job and good credit history.

Quick refinancing: Some of the lenders may only just charge you higher interest rate for this convenience and speed.

Modification: If you choose to just modify your loan, they can just change the interest rate without changing the length of the loan. You can ask your lender for this kind of loan.

Apply online: Sometimes if you apply online, it is quicker than calling their number. In some cases people who apply online are assigned a loan officer and who to reach directly.

A broker: Since brokers do business with many lenders, they can easily help you sort through your options in case you don't know which refinance option to choice.

What lenders may want from you to refinance

◊   Bank or brokerage statement for the last four weeks

◊   Previous year's tax return (or tax returns for the past two years if self-employed or employed at your current job for less than 2 years)

◊   W-2 forms or pay check stubs.

◊   If you are refinancing with a different company other than your current mortgage company, they will need mortgage statement.

◊   Home equity loans or line of credit statements.

◊   If you pay your home insurance by yourself, they will need the insurance statement.

How to spot a bad mortgage lender

◊   If a lender encourages you to falsify your application information to get the loan.

◊   If a lender urges you to borrow more than you need

◊   If a lender pushes you to accept payment terms that you can't realistically meet.

◊   If a lender fails to give you the required disclosures (e.g., APR, rescission rights, etc.).

◊   If a lender shows up at closing with a totally different loan product than you agreed to.

◊   If a lender asks you to sign blank forms. ("It'll speed things up. We'll fill in the blanks later, trust me.")

◊   If a lender denies you copies of documents you signed.

Source: Federal Trade Commission

Make a safe bet

A home should be where you live not just an investment. Most people these days buy a home solely for investment purpose. Sometimes some homes do not go up in value. You should make sure that you do not pay more than 28% of your gross income on your mortgage. It is okay to get that big home as long as you can afford it with room for you to still save some money. The lender always uses your gross income to calculate the amount of home you can afford. You should not let the lender determine your purchasing power. Lenders charge PMI for mortgages over 80%, and there is a way you can avoid this charge. You should try to put down at least 20% of the mortgage to avoid paying PMI (private mortgage insurance) or get the loan that correspond to 80% of your down payment and get a second loan to complete the cost of the mortgage, and get the other 20% loan separate, which is 20-80 or 80-20, they might not have the same interest rate. In this way, you can avoid the PMI. You should ask your lender whether your loan is impounded or not. If your mortgage loan is impounded, that means you will not pay the taxes and insurance for your mortgage by yourself. If it is not impounded, you can pay the taxes and insurance by yourself if you choose to do so. You should know that in some counties, you can pay property taxes yearly and what some lenders do is they will put your money in money market account to generate interest for them, while they turn around at the end of the year and pay your taxes and insurance.

These days, many home buyers put no money down or put down 1 to 2 percent to move in, but remember that low or no down payment allow many home buyers to get in the door, the same reason may help to kick them out of the door. This mostly happen when they cannot afford the payments and they are forced by the lender to sell or move out. Buy a house you will live in between 7 to 10 years. Give yourself some room for errors just in case your income drops or you loose your job. Also give yourself some room for savings when calculating your mortgage payments. There are many website on the internet where you can get free education about home mortgage.

The Lease Option

Getting into home ownership offers many advantages, but if you're just starting out and don't have down-payment funds, leasing, with an option to buy, may be for you. A lease-option agreement can greatly benefit the buyer. This is a method for buying real estate that combines a lease on the property with an option to buy the property at a specified price within a specified amount of time. A lease-option agreement allows you to tie up and control property with a very small investment, and it can provide an opportunity to purchase a home you otherwise couldn't afford.

Although the terms of the lease may be for only a year, they can include options to extend the lease for a number of periods at predetermined rents. When negotiating such an agreement, make sure it includes the right for you to sub-lease the property; often the lease will include a provision from the landlord. In that case, add a statement that the permission from the landlord will not be withheld unreasonably, since it might be possible for you to sublet at a profit.

Home Insurance

You should check your home insurance policy and raise the deductible to $2,500 so that the yearly premium can drop. You should use the insurance only for major repairs. Video tape your home ones a year and put the tape in a safe place like a safe deposit box in the bank or a post office safe box or just put it some where other than your home. In case something happen to your home, you can use the video tape to prove your property claim in case the insurance company try to dispute your claim.

Rental Insurance

Rental insurance is very cheap and you can get rental insurance from your auto insurance company. If you are renting, it is very important. Although many people who are renting overlook this very important concern, you can get rental insurance for about $20 a month. Make sure that the insurance does not cover depreciation value, but replacement value. This is because you don't want the insurance to say you had that TV for 5 years and bought it for $200 and they can only pay you $15 for the depreciation value. If it is replacement value, you will get the current market cost to replace that TV.

Title Insurance Company: Title insurance company will search all records concerning your property and warrant that there are no claims against it other than what they tell you in their title report. Further, if there are claims, the title insurance company will cover the costs of defending your title if it is contested. They are not an appraisal company; as such title insurance company does not establish the value of your property. It simply protects both you and the seller against any claims and sets forth a maximum amount of monetary damages you can expect to recover if a claim is made against you. Whenever you buy property, include title insurance in your purchase. It is valuable protection. Lenders typically require that you purchase title insurance when buying a used home to protect their mortgage loan.

What to do to prevent poor mortgage loans

1. **Fix your credit:** You should check your credit before apply for a mortgage. All you need to do if possible six months before you apply for a mortgage is to obtain copies of your credit report and FICO credit score. FICO score is a three-digit number that's used to make 75% of mortgage-lending decisions. You can order your FICO score on the web for $12.95, at myfico.com.

2. **Look for first-time home buyers' program:** These kinds of programs are sponsored by state, county or city government. They often offer better interest rates and some of them are designed for people with bad credit who want to be home owners.

3. **Get pre-approved for the mortgage loan:** Do not get confused with pre-qualification and pre-approve. Pre-qualification is just to know how much money you can borrow. Pre-approval means you have actually applied for the loan.

4. **Do not borrow too much money:** Some people take out the biggest loan they can take thinking that their income will go up for them to be able to pay. They may not know hidden expenses like property taxes, homeowner insurance, utilities and maintenance.

5. **Shop around for rates and terms:** If you have good credit, you don't want to be given loans that were supposed to be for people with poor credit. You should have idea what the interest is for someone with your type of credit.

6. **Avoid junk fees:** Some lenders charge fees like document preparation fee, credit check fee. Some of these fees are legitimate, but you should shop around and compare charges before you sign for a loan.

7. **Plan for closing costs:** Closing is when you are going to actually get the loan. You will pay for some expenses that day. Expenses like attorney's fees, taxes, title insurance, prepaid homeowner insurance, points and other lenders' fees. Make sure you plan for this and have the money at hand at closing.

8. **Have enough cash in reserve after closing:** You have just borrowed big money and you came up with big down payments and big money at closing, you should make sure you still have some money in reserve after closing for some hidden cost of home ownership.

Car Loans

Car loan is a loan I always tell people to be very careful with especially if they cannot really afford to pay. Most Americans trade in their old cars for new ones simply because the interior is dirty. If your reason for looking for a new car is to impress others, then you need to think twice. It is understandable if your car is parked in a mechanic shop more than you park it in your drive way. You still must weigh your options. I prefer fairly used cars than brand new cars. The biggest killer is leased vehicle. Although it is better for some people if they are able to stay within the allowed mileage. One really terrible thing about financing a new car is that the price of the car drop 10 percent the minute you drive it off the dealership lot. If you spend $1000 to maintain your used car per a year, compare it with a new car that you might pay $400 a month for. I think you will come off better with the used car.

If you want a used car, you may already know what you are looking for, if not there are many websites you can go to these days to find out more about the use car. You can do more research at:

- Autotraders.com
- kbb.com
- nada.com
- Edmund.com
- nhtsa.dot.gov
- autosafety.org
- Lemonaidcars.com

If you find the car you like to buy, you can checkout the history of that use car at carfax.com. From carfax, you can find out if the odometer has been rolled back, if it has been a police car, or if it has been involved in a major accident. The internet has made our lives easier; you cannot take a used car salesman's words just for it anymore. You can go into the internet and check the track record of that model; you can research the vehicle's price, reliability, safety, and history.

Refinancing car Loans

You can renegotiate and refinance smaller loans as well as larger ones. But be careful. Make sure you can benefit from refinancing before you go for it. Suppose you have an auto loan at 9 percent, and your bank is willing to lend you the money to pay it off at 5 percent. This may sound as a good deal. But if a big part of the loan has been paid off, refinancing may not be worthwhile because the new debt is usually paid off over a longer period of time and will ultimately cost more. The more recently the loan was made, the better chance refinancing has to work for you.

Car Leasing

Leasing a car is paying for just the use of the car, it cover the cost of depreciation over the lease period. You as the "Lessee" are expected to maintain the car during the period and when lease is up you can give up the car or exercise your option to buy.

There are some leases called "Capitalized cost reduction," that can help you lease the car without a down payment. All the company "lessor" mostly does is to calculate your payment, which could be based on:

Depreciation + interest + dealer fees = monthly lease payment

Reasons to lease

1. If you need a new car in every 2 to 4 years.
2. If you need a more expensive car, that you cannot afford to buy—because you will pay lower, than if you are financing except if you drive over the specified mileage.
3. If you cannot afford the cash down payment for the new car you want.
4. If your business is buying the car for you—It is tax deductible.
5. If you are not sure you really want the car, but you will like to drive it for 2 to 4 years—Maybe you will choose to exercise your option to buy.

Different between Buying and Leasing

Buying	Leasing
You own the vehicle after payment	You do not own the car after the lease
There are no mileage limit	There are mileage limits
Most manufacturers warranty expire after 3 years	There is manufacturers warranty
Monthly payments are higher than leasing	Monthly payments are usually lower
Most require down payments	Usually—no down payments
Maintenance is voluntary	There are set maintenance
No limits to modifications	Limits to modification e.g. fancy wheels.

WAYS YOU CAN SAVE MONEY

On your search for money, you will feel sometimes like you are running a race, handcuffed and blindfolded.

Ways to save your money

- You should go grocery shopping twice a month and try to use coupons. Don't just shop in one store. Know which store has products that they sell cheaper than others.

- Use newspapers, online advertisements and store flyers to compare prices.

- Try to buy in bulks, especially when they are on sale, and know the seasonal foods, because they will be cheaper in their seasons.

- Grow your vegetables to save money

- Quit smoking if you do, because giving up a pack a day can save you almost $3,000 a year.

- Know each store you shop and where they put the items they have on sale.

- Do not fall for sale pinches. Make buying decisions on your own or by yourself. Be an educated consumer. You should be the one who actually make the decision to make the purchase, you should not get pushed into it

- You can save by buying produce from outdoor stores—They don't incur expenses like regular stores, so they might be cheaper.

- Know each store's specialization like produce, meats, diary, bakeries etc.

- Purchase your airline tickets at least two weeks in advance. And if possible purchase them online with discount online service like priceline.com or hotwire.com.

- Use manufacturer finance company to finance your new car and check out their cash back on line and also take advantage of dealer cash back.

- Choose hobbies that don't require you to spend money.

- If your car is over seven years old and you are not paying car notes on it, consider carrying just liability insurance.

- If you don't have dependents and your spouse is working, cut back on life insurance.

- Help your kids look for scholarship to pay for college education; I have websites you can easily use to look for scholarships on the web in the Scholarship section.

- If your kids are going to private school, move them to public school, because public school is free.

- Buy some stuff from thrift stores and garage sale.

- Compete with yourself when it comes to spending money, don't try to impress anyone.

- Don't spend too much money for anything. Be wise and be an educated consumer.

- If you want to spend, stay below or within your means, and never above your means.

- Use what you have until they wear out—like your cars and clothes.

- Do your repairs by yourself—e.g. home, car etc.

- Do your lawn mowing and maintenance by yourself.

- Do your laundry or dry cleaning by yourself

- When going to store, know what you are looking for. Do not buy base on your impulses. If possible make a list before you leave to the store and stick to the list.

- Find out about a product—the value, the quality, the durability and multiple needs of the product before buying.

- Use the internet; wait for sale, use mail order discounter and discount chain stores—to get products cheap—do comparison shop.

- In some cases, buy the USE versus NEW products. And sometimes you will find out it is better for you to buy the use than buy the new e.g. equipments, cars, boats etc.

- Do not pay credit card according to the minimum required payment—spend what you can pay off at the end of the month. This is how you save and outsmart your credit card lenders.

- Do not have many credit cards. Have one or two credit cards and avoid the ones with high annual fees, high terms and rates. Just get the ones without annual fees and hidden charges like over the limit charges.

- You can really save yourself a lot of money if you pay cash for your purchases. Not for only small purchases, but even cars, boats and homes.

- Quickly pay off your mortgage. There are different ways you can easily pay down your mortgage. If you follow the term of the loan, you will pay three times the purchase price by the time you pay it off.

- Get free banking—There are many banks today that will give you free banking.

- Do not let banks charge you for bounce checks. Avoid bouncing checks.

- Always look at gas prices—Now you can use the internet to check out the prizes of gasoline in any neighborhood you are in. You can do this with most search engines these days. All you need is the Zip code of your area and type it in at yahoo.com, msn.com etc. The costs of gas add up. At the end of the year it can be thousands.

- Buy a gas efficient car.

- If you live in the inner-city, walk to work, walk to take care of some errands.

- If you live on bus line or train—use them.

- Always keep tracks and record your auto maintenance and cost.

- Try to learn how to repair car—like oil change, tune up, tire change and rotation etc.

- Find a mechanic who knows what they are doing and charges reasonable amount for repairs even before you start to have car trouble.

- You should buy needed auto parts by yourself through comparison shop by phone, the internet and have a mechanic help you to do the installation if you cannot do it by yourself.

- Make sure you take good care of yourself—do regular maintenance of your home, car and other valuables to prevent breakdowns.

- Bring your lunch to work and cut back on eating out

- Ride with others to work .i.e. (carpool)

- You can telecommute to work—i.e. use fax, telephone, internet connection if your boss or company allows it.

- Live close to your place of employment to save money and walk if possible to work.

- Work for four days a week and ten hours a day—It will safe you money on commuting.

- If you live where you can ride bike—Ride bike to anywhere you want to go around your neighborhood—It will save you money.

- Before you buy a car, check out the insurance rates to know if it will be high or low.

- You should consolidate your errands to save money and trips.

- You can repair and keep your old car rather than buying a new car.

- It will save you a lot of money if you give up one household car and look for alternate ways to run errands and commute to work.

- Get your insurance with good deductibles and with one company—like car insurance, get $500, home insurance, get $2,500 and major medical that could require surgery, get $1,000.

- If the collision insurance is costing you a year more than 10% (threshold) of your car market value, drop the collision insurance and stay with liability insurance coverage.

- Check out the hospitals that your doctor use and find the cheapest that you can use to visit your doctor.

- You should shop around for the cheapest prices for your prescription drugs.

- You can generate income if you rent out your vacation home i.e. if you have any.

- If you want to rent a house, rent the one that is not for rent. They are usually cheaper.

- If you have space in your home that you are not using, rent it out.

- Live in a neighborhood that is not too expensive.

- To really save money, buy a piece of land and put a motor home in it or better yet sell your home and move into a motor home.

- Get CD's, audiocassettes, video-tapes, books and magazines from the library instead of buying. You can even buy them used.

- Just go to stores sometimes, window shopping and looking at the prices.

- If you are confused, buy the cheapest. Don't get confused with options about what to buy: Many people get cut up with information overload due to options to make choices. These days, you will find it difficult to make choices because there are too many options. Take for example tooth paste, there are many kinds in the market these days. Crests have up to five different kinds and Colgate have more than three kinds. Educate yourself and go for the cheapest.

- Buy generic brand rather name brand. If you are going to use an item once or twice, consider borrowing it.
- Don't catch cabs unless you really have to.
- Stay away from those phone numbers that charge your phone line.
- After looking around in the store, if you see something that you will like to buy, think about how much use or joy you will get from the purchase or use of the product before you make the purchase.
- Know the return policies of the stores you usually shop and retain the documents that will allow you a full refund or exchange. Check out for "after the fact" sales on the items you purchase. Some stores will refund the difference if the price drops.
- Patronize outlet malls. Outlet malls are stores that sell a manufacturer's merchandise direct to the public. They bypass retailer's profits.
- If an item is on sale—Look out for the price not the markdown ("reduced 20 %"). This is because after a markdown, an item can be higher in price than a similar item at another store.
- Shop off season for apparel. You can save even 40% or more on coats, sweaters, suits and pants.
- Before you buy a big ticket item like refrigerator, television etc—first look for stores with "prices that can't be beat" guarantee, then begin comparison shopping in other stores for that item. Never pay full price unless you have no choice, always ask for discount.

You really don't have to pay

A retailer is only allowed to collect taxes—"insofar as it can be done." They cannot collect taxes if you refuse to pay, because the government has not provided lawful money i.e. gold and silver coin. It is clear in Article 1, section 10 of the United States Constitution and by Title 31 section 371 of the United States Codes. It has never been amended. According F. Tupper Saussy, the author of Miracle on Main Street, you can be exempted from sales tax by simply filling out the tax exempt sheet kept behind the counter by retailers. Gold and Silver coins are suppose to be the legal tender by the State government and Kmart, Wal-mart, Target, Rich's-Macy's, J.C.penney's, Kroger, Publix, and many other stores are State registered corporations. Notes money's are provided by Federal reserves which belong to the Federal government. If you listen carefully when you are sued in court for debt payment, some judges usually reads—"This court can only make gold and silver coin a tender payment of debts, this court will accept other forms of money such as Federal Reserve notes or personal checks if voluntarily tendered."

Hotel Security Tip

Some hotels are now installing devices that will prevent your cell phone from working. You should ask at the front desk before you check in if your cell phone will work while you are there or check your cell phone. You can never know while you are in the hotel parking lot and meet an attacker, especially if you are a lady and your cell phone does not work.

Car Rental Tip

If you rent a car, make sure that you check your contract very well before you pick up the car and after you drop off the car. This is because car rental companies also have junk fees. They use all kinds of charges as profit making opportunities. Check the gas options, check the insurance options, check with your car insurance agent before signing for one. If your credit card have insurance program, take advantage of it when you are renting with that credit card—like American Express. If the clerk asks you whether you will like to pay for the gas when you return the car, remember it is always cheaper for you to fill up the car by yourself before you return the car, rather than the rental company charging you for what they claim you used.
Tavel insurance websites
www.AccessAmerica.com
www.Insuremytrip.com

Tax Tip

I have seen some people who have a family of five or six and they claim one or two dependents on their W-4 or withholding allowance form, hoping the government can take off a lot of taxes so that when they file for tax return, they will claim the right dependents. Unfortunately, when they file their returns, they are disappointed when they did not get much refund.

You should know that you are allowed by law to take up to nine (9) as your withholding allowance in your W-4, you normally fill out this form when you are hired. You can always go back to your HR department to adjust it.—You should claim as many as possible, then use itemized deductions when filing. If not you are only giving Uncle Sam interest free loans.

Smooth Deal Auction site Security Tips

- Don't bid on item unless you really want to buy
- You should know your price limit
- Know the market value of the product
- If you have to finance, get financing in advance
- Check the seller's feedback rating
- If it is a car, check the history with the VIN at carfax and compare prices at MSN autos, cars.com, Edmunds.com and autotraders.com.
- Know the hidden charges like shipping and taxes, and if it is a car find out about title and registration.

Identity theft Protection Tips

There are no guarantees, but you can try these measures:

1. Destroy private records and statements. Tear—or, if you prefer, shred—credit card statements, solicitations and other documents that contain private financial information.

2. Empty your mailbox quickly so criminals don't have a chance to snatch credit card pitches. Consider locking your mailbox.

3. Don't carry your Social Security card with you, or any other card that may have your number. Leave your driver's license number off your checks as well.

4. Never leave ATM or gas station receipts behind.

5. Worried about credit card skimming? Pay with cash as often as possible.

6. When making an online purchase, look in the lower right hand corner of your browser window. Make sure you see the icon of a lock that means you're dealing with a secure site. If you don't see one, you'll be safer finding another merchant. Also, check out the Web site privacy policies. Shy away from sites that don't specifically say that they won't pass your name and information around to others.

7. Stick to well-known retailers or sites that others have used to their satisfaction. Use only one credit card for online purchases. That way, if something amiss happens, it'll be easier to spot on your bill.

8. Be more defensive with personal information. Ask salespeople and others if information such as a Social Security number or driver's license is absolutely necessary. Ask anyone who does require your Social Security number—for instance, your insurance company—what their privacy policy is and whether you can arrange for the organization not to share that information with anyone else.

9. Check your credit report at least once a year to look for suspicious activity. If you spot something, alert your card company or the creditor immediately.

10. Investigate credit bureau protection services. For instance, Equifax offers Credit Watch, which alerts you any time a change take place with your credit report.

LED Light bulbs

LED Light bulbs can save you a lot of energy even better savings than compact fluorescent. The LED Light bulbs can last up to ten years and save you up to 90% on what your regular light bulbs are presently costing you every month. Some traffic lights are already using this technology.

Home Energy saving Tips

You can find these tips and more from the department of energy.

Tips for Air conditioning

- Open windows and use portable or ceiling fans instead of operating your air conditioner. Even mild air movement of 1 mph can make you feel three or four degrees cooler.

- Use a fan with your window air conditioner to spread the cool air through your home.

- Use a programmable thermostat with your air conditioner to adjust the setting at night or when no one is home.

- Don't place lamps or TVs near your air conditioning thermostat. The heat from these appliances will cause the air conditioner to run longer.

- Consider installing a whole house fan or evaporative cooler (a "swamp cooler") if appropriate for your climate.
- Install white window shades, drapes, or blinds to reflect heat away from the house.
- Close curtains on south-and west-facing windows during the day.
- Install awnings on south-facing windows. Because of the angle of the sun, trees, a trellis, or a fence will best shade west-facing windows.
- Apply sun-control or other reflective films on south-facing windows.

Do Landscaping for a cooler house

- Plant trees or shrubs to shade air conditioning units, but not block the air-flow. A unit operating in the shade uses less electricity.
- Grown on trellises, vines such as ivy or grapevines can shade windows or the whole side of a house.
- Avoid landscaping with lots of unshaded rock, cement, or asphalt on the south or west sides because it increases the temperature around the house and radiates heat to the house after the sun has set.
- Deciduous trees planted on the south and west sides will keep your house cool in the summer. Just three trees, properly placed around a house, can save between $100 and $250 annually in cooling and heating costs. Daytime air temperatures can be 3 degrees to 6 degrees cooler in tree-shaded neighborhoods.

Some Little things mean a lot

- Replace incandescent bulbs with compact fluorescents.
- Buy a programmable thermostat
- Air-dry dishes instead of using your dishwasher's drying cycle.
- Use a microwave oven instead of a conventional electric range or oven.
- Turn off your computer and monitor when not in use.
- Plug home electronics, such as TVs and VCRs, into power strips and turn power strips off when equipment is not in use.
- Lower the thermostat on your hot water heater; 115° is comfortable for most uses.
- Take showers instead of baths to reduce hot water use.

- Wash only full loads of dishes and clothes.

Don't air-condition the whole neighborhood

- Caulking and weather-stripping will keep cool air in during the summer.
- If you see holes or separated joints in your ducts, hire a professional to repair them.
- Add insulation around air conditioning ducts when they are located in unconditioned spaces such as attics, crawl spaces, and garages; do the same for whole-house fans where they open to the exterior or to the attic.
- Check to see that your fireplace damper is tightly closed.

Pest control tip

Termite Pest Control: If you are having a termite control treatment on your home, make sure the termite control company sign a repair bond with you. This means that they will pay for the repair of your house if your house is damaged by termites. The repair bond really will make them do a good job, because if they don't, they will pay—big time.

BE DEBT FREE

A debt is debt, whether it's margins or mortgages; and debts are all the same, no matter how you try to camouflage 'em. You never get much out of 'em except trouble. On the farm or in Wall Street, if you use the other fellow's money, it cost you a lot more than it's worth.

—Sue Sanders, U.S. Oil Producer

Stop borrowing and Start saving $9 a day

You can choose to start with $9 a day saving by just putting it away into a basket or drawer or automatically into your saving account from your checking. $9 is way less than what most people spend for a meal at a table service restaurant. You can really free up a couple of dollars if you cut back on breakfast, Lunch and dinner, especially eating out. You will for sure able to put away $9 dollars a day and at the end of 30 days you will save $270 and when you do this for 12 months, you will save $3240. Get rid of your debt and start putting money away. It is true that the government are setting bad example by spending the money they don't have. But you don't have to be out of control like the government. If you don't save, you don't have a future—pure and simple. Do not compete with the Jones', just window shopping sometimes, you don't have to bring home everything you like from the store.

Debt has become an American disease. People between 18 and 34 years of age are now spending 105% of their hard earned money servicing debt. These debts are lifestyle debt not really what they must have. These are not student loans, car loans, mortgage loans. We really need to talk to our children about money and debt. We need to go back to the old fashion way of spending, which is "pay-as-you-go"—If you cannot afford it, don't go and grab it.

If it is on your ass, it is not an asset

—*Michelle Singletary*

How to payoff your debt and be debt free

Two steps to become debt free

◊ Take for example, you have a home with a $100,000 balance i.e. on your mortgage, and you are paying the mortgage company $1,000 a month toward your mortgage.

◊ You have other debts i.e. non-home debts; they all total about $1,000 a month. You are paying a total of $2,000 a month in debt.

◊ All these are mortgage payment, credit cards and car note, excluding utilities i.e. light, telephones, water, insurance and groceries.

Step one

◊ Start with the credit cards by paying them off starting with the one with the highest interest rate or better yet consolidate them and start making additional payments above the required minimum payments every month or pay it bi-weekly. They will be paid off in no time.

Step two

◊ Start paying off your mortgage by combining the $1,000 you were paying for non-home debt with the $1,000 you are paying every month for your mortgage. You will now pay $2,000 a month toward your mortgage.

◊ If you divide $100,000 by $2,000, you will have 50 which is equal to 50 months and this will be four years and two months. If you add the interest payments, I approximate it to total five years for you to payoff your mortgage.

◊ You can now include the two years that it took you earlier to pay off your non—house bills, which is 5+2=7. It will take you 7 years to be debt free.

◊ All these may sound over simplified, but it can be done. Many people have done it.

◊ You might ask why should I payoff my mortgage and loose the interest tax deduction? Take for example; if you are in the 30% tax bracket, the government only gives you 30 cents tax break on every dollar you pay on your mortgage interest, which mean you are losing 70 cents on each dollar.

◊ Now that you are debt free, you can create wealth and look forward to obtaining financial freedom. You can now invest the $2,000 a month in an account that protects your principal like municipal bond, I-bond, EE bond or money market saving account. If the account yields 5% interest and compound monthly, you can retire in no time just drawing the interest to live and maintain your living.

Eliminating your credit cards debt

You should know the total amount of credit cards that you owe. Know your creditors and if possible call them and ask for a lower interest rate. Cut the credit cards up, so that you can avoid spending with more credit cards. This is because you cannot eliminate your credit card debt if you keep on spending or charging your credit cards. You should start to carry cash with you or debit card.

You will pay less if you pay with cash or your debit card. This kind of purchases tends to eliminate all kinds of charges you incur with credit card purchases. Make sure your banks do not charge for ATM or debit card usage. You have six options to easily use to get rid of your credit cards debt.

1. Call the credit card company before they send your credit card debt to outside collection agency or call the outside collection agency and negotiate to pay half of the debt. For example if you owe $10,000 ask them to accept $5,000 and you will write the other half off in your income tax as income (form1099). Most credit cards companies will accept this kind of settlement.

2. Transfer all your credit card balances onto one low-interest card.

3. Make a monthly flat rate payoff plan. For example, if you have $5000 balance on your credit that is 2% minimum payment, they expect you to send in no less than $100 this month. Next month, they expect $99.42. The amount will keep going down. Instead, send in $100 every month until the debt is paid off.

4. Pay off the credit card with the highest interest rate first and close the card.

5. Consolidate the credit card debt into one loan.

6. Pay with cash for all your purchases.

How to easily payoff your credit cards debt.

•   The best way is to pay twice or more every month

- The better way is to pay more than the minimum every month
- The good way is just pay them on time every month

For example, if you owe $10,000 on credit cards, it will take about 17 years to pay off if you are just paying the minimum every month. If you pay like $50 dollars extra or pay it twice a month, it can be paid off in less than five years, it depends on how much you send in twice a month.

These are ways you can payoff your mortgage

1. Increase your monthly payment by 10% or so.
2. Just add, for example, 100 dollars or more to your monthly payments
3. Make one month or more extra payment every year
4. Make payments every two weeks instead of monthly.
5. Pay off the balance if you have the money

You can set any of these up in your checking account as schedule transfers or automatic.

Paying off your car loan

Some car loan companies usually calculate the interest first before they calculate the principal. In other words, they will expect your money for the first couple of years to go toward the interest before you start to pay the principal. You should find out from the lender if there is penalty for pre-pay. You can prepay your car loan with penalty, but some car loans are known as "Rule of 78s" or "Sum of digits" This means no need or benefit to you if you send in pre-payment. Ask your lender for you to be sure that your pre-payment go toward your principal. You should make sure that you get a simple interest loan. Some people only hear about the interest rate, but don't ask if the interest is calculated as simple or compound. Always ask for simple interest rate when financing a car.

Twelve ways to avoid debt

1. You should keep a close look on your daily, weekly and monthly spending
2. You should only borrow money for emergencies.
3. You should have a saving plan, so that you can have reserve always.
4. You should change your spending habits the first month you find yourself falling behind on your bills.

5. You should not use credit cards for small purchases.

6. You should shop wisely and seek out very good deals

7. You should avoid impulse buying

8. You should plan and think carefully about what you really want and need.

9. You should always differentiate your needs from your wants

10. You should not ignore your debt, because your debt will not go away. It will increase due to the interest and penalties.

11. You should have your paycheck deposited directly into your account, especially if you know that you don't handle money wisely.

12. You should have money set aside for your credit cards payment and if possible pay them in full.

Credit Cards bill payments guidelines

1. **Immediately pay the minimum:** Pay the bill as soon as it arrive is the safest way, pay the 2% minimum payment as soon as you get the bill will save you late fees. If you have the money, send a bigger payment.

2. **Put proper postage with payment:** send the payment in to your creditor at least a week before the due date with the correct amount of stamp. You don't want your mail to be return because of postage. If you can send it two weeks in advance, the better.

3. **Make sure you write your checks properly:** I know a guy in college who use to put checks in envelope without signing the checks, so that he will have reason not to pay the late fee. Write legible checks and sign them.

4. **Do not forget to use the envelope that comes with the bill:** It is easier if you use the preprinted envelope when sending your bill payment with your signed check.

5. **You can pay by phone:** You can make your payments by phone. These days, some companies, don't charge for this service. This method is quick and easy.

6. **Set your own due date:** You can call the credit card company to ask for a due date that is convenient for you. You can get your bill around your pay days.

7. **Pay online:** Making payment on line can help you to eliminate late fee. With on-line bill pay, you can choose an automatic payment date. This is acceptable by major credit cards issuer.

8. **Call and ask for a fee waiver:** If you mail your bill before the due date, you can call your creditor and ask for a late fee waiver.

9. **Pay by express mail if due date is near:** If your due date is near, you should send your payment by express mail to avoid the late fee.

Credit Counseling Services

You can contact counseling professional organization if you do not know how to get out of debt. Know who the counseling service organization is really working for. Some of them may not have your best interest in mind, since it is the lending companies that will pay them. This is because some of them actually represent business interest rather than yours. Make sure they are professionals rather than amateur. You should be careful with credit fixers, because they usually come up with illegal suggestions like they can give you a new identity and a line of credit for you to start a new credit. You should check out the professional through better business bureaus or even your local consumer protection agency. You can ask other people or find out some testimony about the company. You should always remember that at this point it is really a benefit to the lender if they help you, because they will not want you to file for bankruptcy. They will receive less money if you file for bankruptcy.

Watch out for:

◊   Credit counseling companies that ask for big upfront fees

◊   Check for accreditation of the credit counseling company by checking out if they are affiliated with the Association of Independent Consumer Credit Counseling Agencies or if they are affiliated with the National Foundation for Credit Counseling.

◊   You can know about the company by finding out how much of your monthly payments actually go to your creditor. They may take part of your money and that will delay or make you miss payment. For example, some of them might use your first payment to them as a fee to them.

◊   Find how legitimate they are by finding out if they are trying to make you get better interest rates and settle your debt for little or no much money. This is because some of them give unrealistic promises.

When you really need credit counseling:

◊   When you cannot pay even the minimums on your credit cards

◊   When you are consistently late paying one or more of your regular bills

◊   When you are been chased by creditors and collection agencies

◊   When your efforts to work out reasonable repayment plans with creditors have failed.

How counseling can help your credit

1. This is more acceptable to many lenders than bankruptcy option that will remain in your credit file for ten years.

2. Bankruptcy option is view as a big negative in your credit file all across the board.

3. After you make three to six months minimum payments of the negotiated payments, you will start to look good to some lenders.

4. Some lenders view counseling service as a positive sign that a debtor is taking control of his or her debt.

5. Although your past bad credit still affect your credit score, but it is really a right step toward the right direction.

Bankruptcy—your last resort

If your debt has exceeded your income, maybe you are at a point that you have no other choice but to file for bankruptcy. You can do this yourself if you are really good in filling out forms properly. You can get a kit in the stores like from office depot or OfficeMax or the form from the court house. The better way, is for you to get a good attorney to help your file. You should be careful, because some attorneys might just want to make quick bucks without carefully taken a look at all your debts versus your income. As soon as you file for bankruptcy, it places an automatic enforcement on any repossession, garnishments, foreclosures, and utility shut-offs on you. They can't do anything until the court's decision.

It usually takes few months from the day you file to the day you appear in court to be told that you have received your formal discharge from all the debts. The most important date is the date you file it with the court. The courts usually notify your creditors so that collection efforts, repossession, wage garnishments can stop within a few days. Although bankruptcy will be listed in your credit record, it will be there for 7 to 10 years, it depends on the type of bankruptcy. But debt cosigned by friends or relatives, will be paid by he or she, Bankruptcy will not cover it. And you will not be legally required to pay it.

Personal Bankruptcies

1. **Chapter 7**: This is when all your debts are discharged by the court. If you have assets, they will be sold and use to pay off your credits. Mostly, the liquidation is used to pay off your unsecured debt, like utility bills, credit cards and medical bills. You are still responsible for unsecured debt like child support, student loans and taxes.

2. **Chapter 13**: This will not discharge you of your debt, but just making payment arrangement base on your future disposable income. There will be a trustee you pay to. The trustee will pay off your bills based on the payment schedule they set up with your creditors. Base on your income if you owe $30,000 you may be asked to pay $15,000.

Business Bankruptcies

1. **Chapter 11-Protection:** This is the kind of bankruptcy that most companies in financial trouble usually file. A company files for this bankruptcy protection to give right to the creditors to petition the court to dissolve the company and distribute the available assets. The company is usually sold and abolished to satisfy the debts, if the judge agrees.

2. **Chapter 11-Reorganization:** This is when the judge requires the creditors to accept reduced or deferred payments and set aside all interest charges. This is when the judge really feels that this is for the best interest of the survival of the company. "This option was designed to give struggling companies that might otherwise fail a chance to become profitable and viable.

3. **Chapter 12:** This is a special kind of provision for farmers under the bankruptcy codes. This kind of bankruptcy allows farmers a greater asset-to-debt ratio, because of the requirement for land and equipment to perform their functions.

Exclusions from Bankruptcies

Going bankrupt does not relief you of your IRS debts. This is because the Federal bankruptcy code exclude several categories of debt from the set aside provisions of the law, including

*   Federal and state income tax liabilities
*   Federally backed student loans

- Loans from non-profit organizations
- Secured property loans
- Alimony and child support

Gain Financial Advantage

King of Money Matters

The king of money matters is cash. It is better for you to pay in full than to owe. In other words, cash here mean, pay in full. We all know that many people have been able to get many things done with debt and went on to be successful, but it is shallow Americanism if you can not meet the minimum credit payments and you expect to get rich. If you don't have the ability to pay your debt, it is really shallow. Although it is rear, but if you can afford to pay cash for your home, do it. It will feel better to live in a home that you don't have to worry about your next month rent. No job is secure in the World we live in today. Many people have drowned financially because they couldn't handle their mortgage. Mortgage finance has become a traditional cancer in this society, especially when it comes to people biting more than they can chew. I am saying this because I know a couple who where trying for four years to save about ten thousand dollars for a down payment on a $100,000 home. And by the time they saved up $9,000 for the down payment, they got a lump sum settlement of $90,000 from the insurance company. They went to their realtor, who told them that they can now afford a $300,000 home. For me to cut a long story short, these couples are today struggling from hand to mouth to pay the mortgage.

If you can pay cash for a new car, go for it. The best way for you to do this is do your home work or research. First and foremost, find out the cheapest price the dealership you want to patronize has sold the car in the past that you want to buy. Secondly, find out how long it usually takes before they actually make the sale and the proud owner drives off the dealership lot. Then go for the kill. Someone has done this before. Walk into the dealership and give the salesman a check with about 5% less than they have sold the car before. Tell the salesman that you give them ten minutes to let you drive off, if not the deal is off.

Considering how long it usually takes for them to actually make a sale, they might let you drive off.

If you actually calculate how much it cost you to pay off those groceries you purchase with your credit card, you may have a second thought next time before you use your visa for grocery shopping.

Buying too much stuffs

Many people in the modern World we live in, shop too much. They want to own everything new, especially electronics. All these gadgets that are so call cutting edge technologies get outdated within a couple of years. As the saying goes "Money talks I can't deny. I heard it once, it said bye-bye." When you let that money go, sometimes it takes you twice the effort and time to get the money back. How can you claim to be powerful as a consumer when you buy without the ability to pay back? If you live in a capitalistic society, you should have capital. Having debt, especially debt that you cannot pay back is the worst form of capital, because it limits your power. Do not get me wrong, here; it is okay to have good debt as leverage as long as you can pay it back. Many people complain everyday about their jobs and how they work hard for their money. The question is—why not save and invest your money so that you can make your money work hard for you. You can never get powerful financially speaking if you keep spending and spending. Some people spend to the point they do not even have cash cushion they can fall back on in case they are laid off. For you to accumulate wealth, your first step is to control your wallet. Frugality is cool. It is nothing to be ashamed of. According to Robert Kiyosaki in the prophecy, he define wealth as the number of days you can survive without working, while still maintaining you standard of living.

Ways to make money at your Bank

1. You should eliminate unnecessary service charges at your bank. Service fees vary tremendously. Read your bank statement to make sure you are not charged unnecessarily.

2. You should never let funds accumulate in a non interest-bearing account, such as some checking accounts these days.

3. You should set up a money-market checking account in addition to, or instead of, a regular savings account. They usually out pay more than regular savings accounts, with an interest rate tied to the movement in the prime rate.

4. If you chose a high-interest account, make regular deposits into it. Your paycheck and any other receipts should go to this account. Make direct deposit if possible.

5. Make it consistent—Consistency is very important. It's easier and better to put $85 each month for one year in a high-interest account than to try to come up with a $1,000 deposit once a year.

6. Look for investment alternatives to put your money like CD's, short term government securities, money market mutual fund.

How to cut high cost banking

1. **Check and compare rates online:** Compare banking rates at bankrates.com. You can check by account type and local market in about 30 metro areas

2. **Check with your brokerage firm:** Some of the brokerage firms have better rates than regular banks on money market accounts and regular savings account.

3. **Try online Banking:** Most banks now let you bank on line at little or no charges. This can really make life easier, because you can manage and keep tracks of your finances by monitoring your account online.

4. **Try electronic bill pay:** If you write a lot of checks every month, this is money and time saving for you. And if the service is free the better.

5. **Try free and automated telephone banking:** Most banks have toll free numbers for this service and you can take advantage of it without any cost to you.

6. **Try electronic account:** Some banks will not charge you for anything as long as you use their ATM's, telephone access, direct deposit and many more.

7. **Balance your check book and don't bounce checks:** If you don't bounce checks and balance your check book, you will save yourself lots of money. Some of those bounce could have cost you.

8. **Credit union:** You might want to check out your credit union if you belong to one. They usually give better rates.

"Do what you do, using your talents and abilities because it makes you happy. In everything you do, have a purpose, principle or ideal that you hold dear and will not compromise if the price is right."

—Iyanla Vanzant

Make your savings and investments automatic

You can make your savings and investments automatic by having a schedule money transfers from your checking account to your savings or investment account. These investment accounts include IRA's, stocks accounts, mutual funds account, money market account, Bonds and so on. This will give you a worry free investment and also help you to pay yourself first.

Investing versus Saving

The rich invest their money while the poor and the so call middle class save their money. When things go bad, the rich can tap into their investments to stay above the water. When things slow down or go bad for the poor and middle class they run for their savings to survive. Take for instance, when the poor and middle class are laid off from their jobs. Most financial advisers tell the working class to have eight months living expenses saved up just in case they are laid off. These days those savings might be gone before you know it. This is because with different lay offs, this can be a circle. The rich that don't work for their money make their money work harder for them by taking more and more calculated risk.

Most people are afraid of investments, because they do not take their time to study and understand investments. They only see risks whenever they hear or see investments. The rich on the other hand, see opportunity to increase their wealth. It is very easy for sophisticated investors to know how much of their investments are worth, but most people who are only smart when they are working for someone, do not even know how much their job is worth. You cannot be smart when your daily activities is been regulated by someone else and working hard to make someone else rich.

It really takes financial intelligent to accumulate wealth and gain financial freedom. If you want to really accumulate wealth, you should be—sophisticated, be a financial wizard and be able to take calculated risks. These kind of people study and gather facts before they invest. For example, in the stock market— most sophisticated investors know where to put their money and they know when to bail out. A saver would be alright with a little interest from a CD, while a sophisticated investor will find a vehicle just as save as a CD and with fix return, but three times more return than a CD. This happen everyday due to knowledge and sophistication.

Save

People save when they payless for products and services they buy either directly at the store or indirectly through some professional services. People also save for the future to create wealth either through direct savings in their bank account or some kind of investment. If you are saving on goods and services, make sure you are also saving for the future in your bank accounts and investment, if not, the equation is not balanced up. This is because I know of many people who are very frugal, but have nothing in their bank account or investment to show for it. They are just two pay checks away from homelessness. Their vehicle will break down; they don't have money saved to fix the vehicle.

Savings Accounts

FDIC can only insure up to $100,000 in one savings account. If you are a millionaire, you can have several savings accounts with the same bank or different banks. If you have more than a hundred thousand in one account, you may loose some money if there is any disaster, because the insurance will not cover more than one hundred thousand. In a nutshell, each savings account is insured up to a hundred thousand, and it does not matter how many savings account you open with one bank.

Simple interest and Compound interest

You should always ask any lender about the kind of interest you are getting, don't just fall for the interest rate, know if it is simple or compound interest. If you are borrowing, try to get the simple interest and if you are investing your money, try to get the compound interest.

Simple Interest: Simple interest is applied only to the original principal in calculating the interest.

Annual = A, Principal = P, Rate = R, Time = T

The formula is A = P X R X T

This example is (the principal **times** interest rate **times** number of years). A = ($100 X 6% X 1).

Year	Principal($)	Interest ($)	Balance ($)
1	100.00	6.00	106.00
2	100.00	6.00	112.00
3	100.00	6.00	118.00

Compound Interest: the returns are compounded by reinvesting one period's income to earn additional income the following period. For example at 7 percent compounded annually, $100 will yield $7 the first year. In the following year the 7 percent will be applied to $107 for a return of $7.49. In the second year the principal will have grown to $114.49 that is (100+7+7.49) and another 7 percent for the third year will make the interest $8.01. This process continues with the interest rate being applied to a larger and larger principal. This example assumes that the compounding takes place annually, the process can occur more frequently. $A = P (1 + r) n$

Year	Principal	Interest ($)	Balance
1	100.00	7.00	107.00
2	107.00	7.49	114.49
3	114.49	8.01	122.50

The fact is that compound interest is paid on original principal and on the accumulated past interest

Formula for calculating compound interest:

P is the principal (the initial amount you borrow or deposit)

r is the annual rate of interest (percentage)

n is the number of years the amount is deposited or borrowed for.

A is the amount of money accumulated after n years, including interest.

When the interest is compounded once a year:

$A = P (1 + r) n$

If you borrow for 5 years the formula will look like:

$A = P (1 + r)^5$

This formula applies to both money invested and money borrowed.

Frequent Compounding of Interest:

It is really a different ballgame if interest is paid more frequently; these are just few examples of the formula:

Annually = P × (1 + r) = (annual compounding)

Quarterly = P (1 + r/4)^4 = (quarterly compounding)

Monthly = P (1 + r/12)^{12} = (monthly compounding)

Frequent compounding interest

One time Deposit of $1,000, Earning 10 percent

Frequency	After 1 year	After 5 years	After 10 years
Daily	$1,105	$1,649	$2,718
Monthly	$1,105	$1,645	$2,707
Quarterly	$1,104	$1,639	$2,685
Semiannually	$1,103	$1,629	$2,653
Annually	$1,100	$1,611	$2,594

Know how your bank calculate interest rate

We all know that the Fed has dropped the key federal fund rate by one-quarter point to 1%—which happen to now get to 45 year low—banks responded by dropping their prime rates to 4% from 4.25%. The prime here, you should know determines the cost of many variable-rate loans, such as home-equity lines of credit. This includes rates on adjustable mortgages, new car loans and credit cards loans, as they start to drop. "When you borrow money, do you know how the bank calculates your interest rate? A number of factors enter the formula, ranging from overhead costs to the keenness of competition. The Federal Reserve Board also gets into the act by setting the discount "discount rate," a key short-term rate that banks pay for loans from the Fed. The more banks have to pay, the more they charge. But the dominant element remains the **prime rate.** Other rates are linked to the prime. You may be offered an interest rate that is the prime rate plus 2 percent, for example. This will vary based on how much risk the bank believes there is in making the loan. The prime is the fluctuating rate that banks charge their most credit-worthy corporate customers. In other words, it is the lowest rate available. Smaller firms generally are charged higher rates because they are considered more risky. Back in the early 1980s, the prime zipped to a shocking 21.5 percent, and then slowly declined to 7.5 percent over the decade. It has fluctuated by a few points since then. In late—1996 the prime was 8.25 percent. The prime rate is determined by the supply of money, from various sources, and the demand for loans—the same forces that affect prices of other commodities. If loan demand is heavy and the money supply is tight, interest rates generally will increase. Federal Reserve Banks often influence the market, usually by buying or selling government securities, thereby raising or lowering the money supply; also by setting reserve requirements for member banks and the discount rate. Keep an eye on the prime as it goes up and down. Virtually every daily newspaper lists it in the financial section. Obviously the best time to borrow is when the prime is low. How much is your bank charging you plus the prime? This may be the deciding factor in choosing a bank for your loan."

Try to forecast interest rates

There are fundamental forces that determine how interest rates get set in this economy. Many economists use these factors to forecast the future of the economy. It is very important for you to know how interest rate is set for you to predict which direction it will swing.

You should know these three things:

- Household savings. The money saved in the economy—Which include you, the money you save.

- The demand by businesses for this money for them to finance new plant construction, buy new equipment, buy supplies and so on.

- The government demand for funds and the net supply of funds by the government.

Factors that causes inflation

- **The department of labor employment report:** Most economists look at this on the first Friday of every month. When it shows that everyone has a job, they may be nervous. "This report estimates the number of workers added to the non-farm payroll. (The government counts farm workers separately because the work is so seasonal and fluctuates wildly.) This report is seen as a harbinger of inflation and, thus, higher interest rates if it shows tightening labor markets that could lead to increased pressure for higher wages. This is particularly true when the overall rate of unemployment is low."

- **The quarterly worker productivity report:** This is when workers succeed in making more things faster, which means unemployment is low.

- **The employment cost index (ECI):** This shows if employers have increased wages to keep their workers.

- **The gross domestic index (GDP):** It is use to measure how much our domestic economy is producing.

Inflation measurement is really done with:

- **The consumer price index (CPI):** The price of a basket of goods and services that consumers purchase.
- **Producer price index (PPI):** PPI is a predictor of what will happen at the consumer level in the future.

General economic trends determine the overall interest rates in the economy, lenders are increasingly using what they call risk-based pricing in consumer lending, ranging from credit cards to car loans to even your home mortgage.

Know when your money will double

There is an easy way to approximate how long you must hold your investment at a fixed return to double your money. It is called the Rule of 72. Divide 72 by the percentage of the return, and you get the number of years it'll take to double. For example, you have a mutual fund paying 6 percent. Without adding to it (just letting interest compound), you'll have twice as much in 12 years. Conversely if you have $1,000 ready to invest that you want to double—and you know you'll need the money in, say, **10 years—divide the years into 72 i.e. 72 divide by 10.** You'll need an investment vehicle that gives you at least a 7.2 percent rate of return. It works on any sum of money.

Ways to simplify your finances

1. **Direct Deposit:** Using direct deposit will make it easier for you to manage your finances. It is better than standing in line at the bank to cash your check. Worst of all standing at a check cashing center to pay those charges they charge to help you cash your check.
2. **Overdraft Protection:** This is very important to protect your checking account and your name from all those bounce checks that might happen. Those bounce checks can cost you from $10 to $100 a year, and that is a lot out of your pocket.
3. **Personal finance software:** Quicken or MSN Money can give you an easier way for you to keep track of your finances. You can easily see your debt, budget and your payments.

4. **Reminder set up:** With reminder functionality feature in your personal finance software, you will not pay late fee on your credit cards again. This is if you use this functionality. The online bill payment system also has this functionality called bill reminder.

5. **Credit cards consolidation:** Consolidate your credit cards debt, especially if you have more than two. This will help you not to forget and pay late fee.

6. **Consolidate all your accounts:** Put all your accounts with one bank, so that you can easily see then and keep track—like your Mutual funds, IRA's, brokerage accounts.

7. **Have a good filing system:** set a filing system that you can easily locate your bills like a filing cabinet which you can get from any office supply company or you can buy Homefile.

8. **Automatic bill pay:** This will save you a lot of headache, especially if you have many bills to pay every month. There are three ways you can do this:

   • Direct payment
   • Credit card charges
   • Online bill payment

CREATE WEALTH

"Once criticized for urging people to make money, the great minister, author of *Acres of Diamonds* said, "money printed the bible, money builds your churches, money sends your missionaries, and money pays your preachers, and you would not have many of them, either, if you did not pay them." The person who says he wants to be poor usually suffers from guilt complex or a feeling of inadequacy. He's like the youngster who feels he can't make A's in school or make the football team, so he pretends he doesn't want to make A's or play football."

Common People are creating wealth

Common people who work every day just like anyone else are creating wealth with their earned income through perseverance, good planning, hard work and self discipline. Most of the wealthy did not inherit their wealth, win the lottery or simply lucky to acquire their wealth.

They have simple lifestyle living, by being frugal and managing their money very well not to live above their means. You can do the same by focusing your time and effort on these things:

1. Learn to live below your means or income

2. Focus your time and energy on areas that you know you can excel in terms of wealth creation

3. Choose financial security over social status. Do not rent your lifestyle.

4. Plan to save rather than spend

5. You should target the right opportunities in terms of shopping, career opportunity, doing businesses and investing.

Penny Pinchers

Penny-pinchers have being accumulating wealth by shopping carefully and avoiding mortgages and car loans if possible.

- They avoid many things that frivolous spenders do.
- They are savers and not spender.
- Many of them are millionaires in your neighborhood, and you do not know them as millionaires.
- They are very frugal
- They avoid debt as much as possible.
- A penny pincher can easily differentiate between owe and own, asset and liability.
- They wait for items to go on sale
- They use coupons most of the time, especially when the item is also on sale. For example, if you have a coupon in your organizer and you find an item on sale for 25% off, you can easily get that item for 50% off with coupon. What a way to save your money.

Fast Track to wealth creation

If you want to create wealth quickly, you should not get use to the 9 to 5 routine that most corporate followers and mediocre follow. It is very hard and it takes longer time frame to accumulate wealth while working for somebody. You have to have a realistic plan, if not, you will be placed in the plan that is already created by some corporate executive. In fact, the fast track can easily be accomplished with a concrete plan. It will allow you to write your job responsibilities or description rather than someone else writing it for you. Most good job descriptions are job descriptions where by you report to someone or people that you even make more money than and them firing you will not cripple your life. If you report to the so call bosses that you are afraid of every day, you are not on the fast track. People on the fast tracks are investors, inventors, writers, actors, musicians, entrepreneurs, politicians to name a few. The people in these areas make more than their bosses or customers, and some of them can even have residual income.

Do it—Wealth Creation

Many businesses started with just an idea. Most start-ups or new companies are started with a startling idea for a product or service. If you really don't know exactly where you may get that big break, just follow your idea and remember there is no perfect time to get started. The easy way is to go with your passion and see where it leads you to.

When Masaru Ibuka in 1945 started a company in Japan in a bombed-out Tokyo department store, he did not really know what kind of business he was going into. He just had an idea that later gave birth to Sony Corporation.

Bill Hewlett and Dave Packard—founders of Hewlett-Packard had the same problems in the 1930s with vague goals—they started with bowling foul-line indicator, a clock drive telescope and they try urinal flushers. They later branch into profitable area in electronic equipment, computer products and printers.

Paul Galvin started out repairing, then later manufacturing battery eliminators for sears radios and later started Motorola.

Bill Gates—Who is a college dropout, had ideas about information access.

Michael Dell—who is also a college dropout, had ideas about mass production and quick delivery and support of computers to businesses and home users.

Dave Thomas (Founder of Wendy's) wrote a high-school term paper on being a cook and owning a restaurant and he made his ideas come true.

Three secrets for wealth creation

1. Come up with what you want
2. Check out all the available opportunities
3. Make a plan to do it to get the right result

What kind of business is better for you?

Sole Proprietorship—It is a liability company because it is an unincorporated business that is owned by one individual.

Limited Liability Company

The limited liability company (LLC) has become the most popular business form for smaller, privately held companies throughout the United States. With its tax benefits, financial flexibility and personal legal protection from business debts, it offers business owners a safer and more convenient way to do business. "An LLC can have an unlimited number of members (owners) while a subchapter S Corporation is restricted to no more than 75 shareholders."

S-Corporation (Sub-Chapter)
The S Corporation is a pass-through tax entity—this means that the income or loss generated by the business is reflected on the personal income tax return of the owners.

"An eligible domestic corporation can avoid double taxation (once to the shareholders and again to the corporation) by electing to be treated as an S corporation. Generally, an S corporation is exempt from federal income tax other than tax on certain capital gains and passive income. On their tax returns, the S corporation's shareholders include their share of the corporation's separately stated items of income, deduction, loss, and credit, and their share of nonseparately stated income or loss."

An S Corporation is simply a (Closed) C Corporation (also known as a standard business corporation) that files IRS form 2553 to elect a special tax status with the IRS. The articles of incorporation that are filed with the state are same whether a corporation is a C Corporation or S Corporation.

C—Corporation (Closed or standard)
A C Corporation is a separately taxable entity. The profits and losses are taxed directly to the corporation. No more taxes on dividends.

You can ask yourself these questions to see if you might find your passion

1. What ways can I make a living from what I consider fun and challenging?

2. What is it that people will pay for that is not now available? In this case, start by looking at the ways things are done and the problems people are dealing with everyday, then seek solutions to the problems. This is how Mr. Smith started Federal express with overnight delivery service. Some people wanted their mail to be in their destination the next day, but it was just a problem until Fred Smith came up with Federal Express now FEDEX. This was a niche.

3. How can certain products and services be done less expensively and more value added? This can be products and services of individuals, small or big companies—their inefficiencies, availabilities, multiple uses, and repositioning for better usage.

Positive enforcers for wealth creation

Mindset: You have to have a positive mind set to do anything that involves invention, risk taking and success. Most of the inventors took some form of risk or the other at the beginning, but they believe in their ability to succeed. It is hard to succeed with a negative mindset.

Attitude: You also have to have a positive attitude in dealing with people. This is because people will use or need your product one way or another. Keep in mind that "attitude is everything." Be optimistic.

Focus: You should concentrate seriously on your plan and sense of direction. Even in the stock market, Focus investors make more money than diversified investors. Take for example, $10,000 each is given to two investors, one is a focus investor while the other is a diversified investor. Maybe they both have the same knowledge and experience about the market movement, but the diversified investor doesn't know when to take a bigger risk. They both know of a stock that has a possibility of moving up 25% by next week, due to some political, technical and others fundamentals that move the market, the focus investor, invest 50% of the money while the diversified investor invest 5% of the money on that particular stock, it is obvious that the focus investor will make more than the diversified investor will make.

Determination and persistent: You have to be determine and persistent in other for you to create wealth. You have to be a smart salesman. You have to be a salesman who never want to take no for an answer. Many doors will be closed on your face, but you can never give up if you want to succeed.

Location and Timing: You should always try to calculate right. If you get the wrong answer, you did not fail. You learn from it and move on. It is just that you did not get the result you were looking for. You have to position yourself to be at the right place at the right time.

Execution and Action: Some people will say they are going to do something again and again year after year. There are certain things you got to do to succeed. You cannot pass an exam if you did not take the exam. You cannot win if you did not play. If you want to win, just play.

Creativity: Some successful expects always say that life is not that hard, all it take is good attitude and a little creativity, you will be surprise to see yourself moving toward the right direction of productivity and prosperity. You have to be resourceful.

Passion and desire: Some people are afraid to pursue their dreams. You find a lot of people who are in occupation they dislike, but they are in it because they fill they will not succeed in their passion and desire. It is a shame to start to regret when it is all said and done.

Negative enforcers for wealth creation

Negativity: If you are feel very negative from the start either about what you have to begin with or what the result will be, you will not succeed in most cases. You have to build a positive faith to easily make it. Don't be a pessimist.

Frustration: If you try and did not succeed don't get frustrated; because if you do, you are not helping the situation, you are only setting yourself up for more failures. It is okay to be nervous or have cold feet, but in other for you to succeed, you have to do your research very well, get prepared and keep on keeping on.

Problems and impossibilities: You have to view problems as opportunities to re-group and come up with new sense of directions. Look at problems as crossroads and just a step backward that can give you an opportunity to take two steps forward.

Disbelieve: You have to believe in yourself even if nobody did. If you don't believe in yourself, you already fail before you start.

Procrastination: Stop postponing what you can do today till tomorrow. "Just do it."

Wealth creation Scenario

If for example you invented a product—may be a t-shirt you designed and your profit from this shirt or blouse is about $1. In the state of Georgia, we have about 7 million people and let say that about 1 million people buy the shirt or blouse in Georgia that will automatically make you a millionaire. If the shirt is so good that the price goes up or your profit from each is $5 that will give you 5 million. We have not yet reach out to the other states. There is pretty of money to make everybody rich. You should be resourceful, creative and persistent. We are our worst enemies, when it comes to wealth creations. This is because we have reasons why we cannot rather than why we should. These reasons could be fear, and may be other reasons not to step out of our comfort zone.

> When the product is right, you don't have to be a great marketer.
>
> —Lee Iacocca

Be optimistic, positive and hopeful: Being optimistic, positive and hopeful are very important in achieving your goals. This is because it does not matter how a belief seems to someone else, if it is true to you, it will prevail. If you think you will make it or you believe you will not make it, you are right. It is all in the state of your mind. Any belief that does not promote prosperity will obstruct prosperity.

Sometimes looking for money first is like putting the cart before the horse. Look for something you are passionate about and go after it. Just chasing dollars can keep you behind prosperity. Look for what you love to do and what people need.

You are never depressed because you are broke; you are broke because you are depressed. Some miserable rich people have been known to say that money does not buy happiness. You should not listen to what they are saying. You can be rich and happy at the same time. Although as you already know not every rich person is happy, just as not every poor person is happy. It is hard work being rich, but it is harder work being poor. Although money is not everything, but it can sometimes buy you some happiness.

There is nothing wrong if you love the source of money, but don't love money itself, because the love of money is the root of all evil. Worshipping money can lead to permanent destruction. Some people might tell you that "God don't like rich people much." This is not true, because the scripture is against, greed, ungodly and materialistic—and not all rich people have these traits. Some poor people have these traits.

> *I'd rather be a failure in something that I love than a success in something that I don't.*
>
> —*Gorge Burns*

SECRETS TO FINANCIAL SUCCESS

It does not matter if you are making minimum wage or not—you can create wealth if you follow the success secrets outlined below. This is because you will come out a winner in the long term. These secrets are very much applicable to the kind of lives we live today.

1. **You should have a plan:** You should have a plan about what you want and how you are going to get it. And if you tithe, how much you are going to pay for God's work first, then pay yourself and save.

2. **Start growing your wallet:** For every one hundred dollars you earn, take out for use but ninety, this means you save ten. You should save about ten percent of your monthly income. Look for a good saving account with very good compound interest and make sure they accrue frequently. For example an orange savings account offered by: www.INGDirect.com—which is ING Bank—a member of FDIC.

3. **Control your expenditures:** All that each of us calls our 'necessary expenses' will always grow to equal our income unless we protest to the contrary. We have to differentiate between our wants and needs. "Confuse not the necessary expenses with thy desires."

4. **Make your money multiply for you:** Put your money to work for you. Seek out an investment that can give you a continuous stream of income whether you work or travel.

5. **Guard your treasures from loss:** Always seek where to put your money and make sure you protect your principal, because you don't want to exit an investment short. Invest mostly where your principal is safe. For example Bonds, CD's and money market accounts.

6. **Make your home a profitable investment:** You should own your home paid off. There are ways you can easily pay off your home. Make sure you ask your mortgage or finance company if there is penalty for prepay and if there is non, increase your monthly payment by 10%, maybe just add $100 dollars to your monthly payments or make one month extra payment every year or make payments every two weeks instead of monthly.

7. **Insure your future income:** You should provide in advance for the needs of your growing age and the protection of your family. Save for the future, especially your retirement and your kid's education.

8. **Increase your ability to earn more:** you have to be stronger and definite. Know what you want to do and just do it. Learn to become wiser and more skillful. You should go back to school if necessary.

Employment Security

Many parents tell their children everyday to get good education from good schools and get a secure job with a big corporation. How secure are these jobs these days? If you have your own business, you will not worry about company downsizing and layoffs. It is true that everyone can get rich. "The problem is most people would rather do things the hard way." In most cases, it is all they know. "Many will work hard all their lives living below their means; invest in things they do not understand; work hard for the rich rather than work hard to make themselves rich; and they do what everyone else is doing rather than do what the rich are doing." If you really look around, there are no secure jobs anymore and most people who seek secure jobs are not really successful. Take for example, my friend who has a high school diploma was given a factory job for $20 an hour and he quickly grab it, while my other friend who also has a high school diploma was given an opportunity to sell homes for a builder in different subdivisions, he accepted. This kind of job, I look at as an opportunity job. Guess who actually made more money when they were both very good at what they were doing. The real estate friend of mind could make $30,000 in a very busy month, while the factory guy was waiting for his $2,500 take home at the end of the month. People do not want to take chances; they just want that comfortable job with steady check biweekly. All this does is making someone else plan their lives for them and they end up with car notes and big mortgages and stuck on that job for life. At the end they start to wish they had known.

> Life is long if it is full

> —Seneca

Plan and budget

You have to come up with a plan. "A plan is your bridge to your dreams." "Those who plan their lives appropriately don't have to worry about their jobs running to India or China." Rich people do not look at their income statements; they look at their balance sheet. In other words, it is the poor people that mostly focus on their income and expenses. The rich focus on their assets and liabilities. And the rich make sure they have more assets than liabilities.

You should always plan and budget realistically. Make sure you can track your spending or purchases. Always weigh your options toward achieving your goals.

Determination + Goal setting + Concentration = Success

You can look at it this way as well.

Know what you want + weigh your options + make a choice and go for it, then arrive at your destination.

Stay away from bad debt—especially debt that you cannot deduct the interest from your taxes—for example: Credit cards, car loan and so on. You should try to acquire debt that the interests are tax deductible like student loans, business loans and mortgages.

Know your financial basics

1. **A balance sheet:** Summarizes your financial status at a given time.
2. **Income statement:** Helps you to understand where your funds originate and where they go.

3. **Cash flow Statement**: Helps you track your cash receipts and payments.

    If you do not feel yourself growing in your work and your life broadening and deepening, if your task is not a perpetual tonic to you, you have not found your place.

    —*Orison Swett Marden*-

Seek financial security rather than secure job

You have to have a goal before you can come up with a very good plan and as you achieve the goals, you keep coming up with bigger and better goals—mostly refer to as milestones. Start slowly by doing the easier tasks first and gradually move to the next level and more difficult tasks. You should praise and reward yourself as you accomplish those tasks and get to the next milestone. You have to know how to play the game call life. Any where you want to go; you should know what to pack for the trip before you embark on the trip. If you say that you are going to do something, just saying it is not good enough. You have to do it especially if it can be done. In fact, with God on your side, you can do anything. Take for example, if you say that you will like to pay off your debt in twelve months, you should come up with a realistic plan to have your debt paid off in twelve months. After you figure them out, then you can walk your talk.

Meditation: Most of the highly productive people take time everyday to meditate, because it reduces their stress level. If you cannot take time to meditate, then take time to pray. You can do this about three times a day for about fifteen minutes each, even at your desk and you will be surprise at your energy and productivity.

> When you are dependent, you lack control. When you are independent, you gain control.

> —Jesse B. Brown
> Krystal Investment management

The poor and most middle class in America only have one source of income and that is the income that they get from their employer. Although America is an employer driven society, but in reality, it is an employee made society. In the long run, in most cases, it is the employees that actually suffer. This could be due to layoffs, downsizing, and when a company relocate or move overseas. The rich and the wealthy always get income from different sources, even the corporate top executives, like the CEO's, CFO, chairman and president. Apart from the unbelievable salaries, they have packages like stocks and bonds, which give them portfolio income. Apart from the top corporate officials, if we look at the rich very carefully, they get income from other sources in most cases. Take for example, the television actors. Most of them are also movie stars, Broadway actors, musicians, and they own several businesses and investments. In most cases, it has been the poor and middle class that have been stocked in the only one earned income job. The poor and the middle class are now finding out that the job they have is not secure, but most are one check away from homelessness. One check does not cut it for them any more. As a result, the children surfer, because they are in daycare all day while mom and dad are busy working to bring home half a loaf. Some people put their careers ahead of their families. Almost every house nowadays are two income families, both husband and wife have to hold down jobs to make ends meet. The neglect and abandonment of the kids, surface later in their life and their behaviors, because their parents dropped out on them. We forget that at the end, it is family that will really count. The question is—Where is our priorities? We cannot really blame any one for this kind of behavior. This is due to the fact that one of the keys to longevity is for you not to only have a wallet, but always have something in your wallet. Some people may say that money cannot buy you happiness. This is one of the biggest lies that the rich started to keep the poor quiet.

We can look at the educational system. It is focus on training people to go out and gain employment. The educational system is mostly focus on making people employees, not employers. We all know that being employee makes you to be dependent, not independent. And we also know that you can never be truly happy when you are not free. Are you held hostage by your employer? Don't worry help is on the way, just read on. As most parents always preach to their kids, go to school and get good education, then get a secure job with a big corporation. We have learned again and again that "secure job" is like driving a problem car in a slow-lane. It will take you longer to get to were you are going and maybe you might not even get there at all. Even worst, you might completely be broken down on your way.

- Learn how to move from your present level to your desire destination with good planning and commitment.

- Learn how to pay those bills that never stop coming. Always live within your means and remember that those bills will come even though you are dead.

- Learn to make your life easier with technology. We live in an information age, where many people now have their offices in their wallets, waists, cars and homes.

Before ERISA was passed, ERISA (the Employee Retirement Income Security Act of 1974) you could most certainly have a secure employment, but sorry, the corporations have become so strong that they have taken over the government. You should seek financial freedom rather than employment security. We live in a World where people bash the public school system, because they become smart after they graduate from public school.

> *When riches come, they come in such abundance that you begin wondering where they've been hiding all the lean years.*

> *—Anonymous*

Do you owe or own?

Most people can gauze their average income if they have dependable employment. Sometimes, apart from fixed income, some people do have variable income, although majority of people who have been able to plan well with either income, retire rich and happy. For example, if you earn $50,000 now, depending on your age and lifestyle, you may need one million in your saving at retirement. And don't forget the biggest financial cancer most people face today is debt. It can really be controlled with the right knowledge and planning.

First and foremost, you should really differentiate owe from own. You can easily do this if you look at the different between your assets and your liabilities. The media has confused most consumers as to the true definition of ownership. If a product is rented to eventually be owed by you in your name does not really mean that you own it. It is better for you to look at it as you are renting it to eventually own it, which you know to be true. The Banks and financial industries are always looking for catching words that make the consumers feel like they are benefiting. The truth of the matter is that if you don't have the title in your name, you do not own it, you owe on it, and renting to own. The ownership definition by the media is more or less like a temporary assignment. The product is listed in your name as the borrower in the lenders database. The credit cards companies, Banks, and financial institutions has classified debt has OWN. This is because it sounds better for their business and advertising. They have successfully twisted the definition to their favor. If you are financing a product, you are renting to own, not own. You are just renting a lifestyle.

Balance Sheet

In order to accumulate wealth, you have to work on increasing what you have in the left column, to make sure they are more than what you have in the right column.

A Sample of a Personal Balance Sheet

Assets		Liabilities	
Cash at hand	$	Bank Loan	$
Bank Accounts	$	Credit cards debt	$
Paid off Car	$	Property taxes	$
Household goods	$		
Equity on House	$	Total Liabilities	$
Total Assets	$	Net worth = Assets minus Liabilities	

Your Bank's balance sheet

Your bank's balance sheet is no different from other companies' balance sheet or your balance sheet. In fact you can look at it just as you can look at your personal balance sheet. It has assets on the left column and liabilities on the second. Take for example, the home you live in that you are financing, it is an asset in the bank's balance sheet because it will fall on the left while it will fall on the right as a liability in your balance sheet. If you have more items listed on the right side than on the left side, you might be in trouble. This is because the rich, like your bank, have more items listed on the left. If you want to accumulate wealth and gain financial freedom, you should focus on having more items listed on the left side of your balance sheet and if possible leave the right column which is the liability column blank.

Wealth building effect

Some people refuse to pay off their mortgage, because of the tax deduction. I think it is better to pay off your mortgage, if you can afford to do so as quickly as possible. This is because Uncle Sam only gives you 30 cents break on your taxes for every dollar you pay, if you are in the 30% tax bracket. This means that you are losing 70 cents on each dollar for the mortgage interest deduction. If someone tells you that paying a dollar to get 30 cents is good investment, tell them to redo their math. It is better to pay it off than giving Uncle Sam 30 cents from every dollar of the interest you pay—talk about tax free loan and making the mortgage company richer.

- "An extra payment of $100 applied to a 9%, 30-year fixed $100,000 mortgage will save you $75,394 in interest."

- Adding just 15% to your monthly mortgage payment can cut 10 to 15 years off the average mortgage.

- More than half of all the money you make in your lifetime will go towards taxes, debt payments, and fees.

- Average homeowners stay in their homes for 7.1 years from (National Association of realtors®). With an average 6% mortgage, they will sell their homes still owing over 90% of the principal. If they continue this trend, they will NEVER pay off a home in their lifetime.

Banks, credit card companies, mortgage companies and finance companies encourage debt. Credit card companies try to get college students as early as possible to have credit cards. This is also attractive to most consumers because they can use credit cards to pay for groceries and rent nowadays. Some companies now charge penalty fees to customers who have no balance on their cards. These companies will require a credit card holder to pay minimum of 3% of the outstanding balance. If you make the minimum payments in a $3,900 balance at 18%, it will take you 42 years to payoff and you will pay a total of $14,530.44. Credit card companies like Banc One now want people to own their credit card against 40% of their 401k. This is terrible, throwing your future in a black hole.

Each dollar you pay pass or above the required minimum payment on any debt you owe will earn you a profit that is equivalent to the interest rate that the debt charges. "If you can pay an extra $100 towards the balance of a credit card that charges 15% interest, you are getting wealth building effect of earning 15% annually on that $100. The more you prepay against a debt balance, the more you save in interest."

> It is better to live rich than to die rich

—Samuel Johnson

Use financial institution and create wealth

Since we all know how debt has become the biggest cancer in our lives, we can eliminate them.

- Find where the wallet is leaking with proper budgeting
- By determining which debt to pay off first.

We can accelerate our debt payoff—Most financial institutions hate this because you are using them instead of them using you. You should always find out from the bank or financial institution if there is a penalty for prepay before you accelerate your payments.

- You can also accelerate your retirement planning and wealth building

> "A good debt is not as good as no debt."
>
> —Chinese proverb

Good debt versus bad debt

Good debts are debt you acquire as part of investment **for your future**. Bad debts on the other hand are debts you acquire **against your future**. If you know that you cannot afford to pay for something and you buy it anyway, it is bad debt, including a house, i.e. if you cannot afford to make the payments. Good debts are deductible interest, these are interests you can deduct from your taxes, and bad debts have interests that are personal, you cannot deduct them from your taxes. Bad debts really are lifestyle debt that many people are involved in today. These could be debt like credit cards, car loans, personal loans and more. Many people in bad debts knew bad debts all their lives and it is difficult for some of them to change. After they have been hurt badly by debt, they then think that debt is totally bad. Debt can be a very good leverage if you use it wisely, especially good debt. So, not all debts are bad.

Good debts are debts that you accumulate on goods and services that increase in value overtime. Your car is bad debt, because it decreases in value the moment you drive it out of the dealer's lot. Good debts are debts like student loans, which can give you a better position in life and you can deduct the interest that you payback from your taxes. Home loans are good debts because most of the time your home will appreciate in value and you deduct the interest you are paying yearly from your taxes. Business loan is also a good loan.

A simple formula to becoming financially independent
- You should have specific goals
- You should have specific time to achieve your goals
- You should write down your goals

- You should develop a plan to achieve your goals
- You should decide what price you are willing to pay to achieve your goals
- You should think about your goals every day you wake up.
- You should take action and just pursue your goals.
- You should reward, praise and encourage yourself at every milestone you reach.
- You should not be discouraged if you fail, revise your goal and do it again. If you succeed in reaching your goal, set another goal and start again because life is a journey.

Where is your money going wrong?

You should adjust your daily, your weekly and monthly behavior. This is very important if you really want to get out of debt and create wealth. Do not confuse your needs with your wants. If you cannot afford to purchase a product, don't purchase it to be like the Jones's. According to the American Demographics, "The average American will spend $1,860,000 on goods and services in his or her lifetime." The sad part of this is that most Americans make their purchases with credit cards. Credit card companies, Banks and financial companies encourage indebtedness, because they generate so much profit from them. They even market credit cards to students and young adults. Credit cards can now be used in fast food restaurants, and to even pay for groceries. If you truly look at the interest and calculate how long it takes most people to pay it off, you will agree that it does not worth it. You can make a simple chart like the one below to track your budget every month if you cannot afford to buy Microsoft money or Quicken.

A Sample monthly budget (fill in the blank)

Monthly Budget	December	
	Actual Expenses	Expected Expenses
Total Monthly Income =$2000		$1500.00
Saving (Pay yourself first)	200	$100.00
Credit Cards	150	100.00
Phone		50.00
Water		40.00
Light		50.00
Cable		
Food		

Monthly Budget	December	
	Actual Expenses	Expected Expenses
Internet		
Rent		
Clothes		
Automobile		
Insurance		
Recreation		
Medicals		
Miscellaneous		
Surplus/Shortfall		

Note: These items are not written in order of importance

Slim line your monthly expenses

- Turn off the light when no one is in the room.
- Don't leave your computer on all the time.
- Use cold water to wash your plates and clothes
- Down grade your high-speed Internet service to dial-up.
- Cut back on cable service or if possible give it up or just go with the basic.
- Get rid of long distance on your wire line phone and get free long distance on your wireless phone.
- Make most of your wireless phone calls late in the evenings or night.

Try to predict the future

In everything you do, you should try to predict where the wind is blowing. Take for example, the dotcom era—many internet stocks were moving up $20 or more in a day without any good company fundamentals. Some smart people knew when to buy the stocks and they sense when it was time to bail out.

On the other hand, many smart people who can look at the past, present and then predict the future were able to see that trouble may arise. What have you got to loose if your prediction is wrong? They can chart what might happen in the future with social security, health care industry, and the stock market.

First and foremost, social security is paid now at 62 for early withdrawals and 65 to be fully eligible. The number of workers that are currently supporting one retired worker is about 100 to 1. And as more and more people go into retirement, this might change significantly, in that by 2018 it will be about 5 workers supporting 20 retirees. In addition, when it comes to longevity, 1 white woman go on and enjoy the social security benefits one way or the other of 10 black men, because most of them do not live enough to collect social security.

Secondly, look at the healthcare industry and how it is booming, because many baby boomers are getting sick. The healthcare professionals are highly in demand. The supply of medical professionals are less than the people seeking medical attention, but around 2020, the baby boomers must have all retired and couple with advance in medicine, many people might not seek medical attention as they do now. The number of medical professionals will outnumber the people seeking medical attention.

The third is the stock market that has been going up over the years, although it fluctuates in its movement. There are more mutual funds companies today than publicly traded companies on Wall Street. As the baby boomers retire in 2020, they will be looking at the market that has forced them to be investors, since that is what the system and the mutual funds arena has forced them to be. As you know many of these people only invest in 401k, mutual funds and other retirement's plans. What will happen when they sit at home watching how the market fluctuates up and down and how their money going is doing for a period of time, they will not be able to stand it. The result is that they will start taking out their money, because they can not watch their nest egg gambled with. As they pull out their money, the market will be going down. The market cannot go up if accumulations do not exceed distribution. What I am saying here is that the market is driven up by buyers not sellers.

Quitters never win and winners never quit.

—Anonymous

Play to win

Because you are in the game does not make you a player. When we want to be good and be perfect, we learn through practice and we become masters in the craft we indulges in. To be a true player, you have to be good in what you do. Average is not good enough today, in the world we live in. If you are not a good driver, you are a danger to yourself, your passengers, and others on the road. Winners are people who are good in what they do. It is okay to be a player, but play to win.

Income Statement

In order to accumulate wealth, have a balance and surplus budget; make sure you have more in the income section than in the expenses section. You should be familiar with how to compute and read your income statement. You have to make sure that your expenses do not exceed your income, although this is not the case with most people.

A sample income statement

Income	
Salary	$
Interests	$
Dividends	$
House Appreciation	$
Other Income	$
Total Income	$
Expenses	
Deductions from salary	$
Housing payments or rent	$
Utilities (electric and water)	$
Phone	$
Heating	$
Auto	$
Insurance	$
Foods	$
Clothing	$
Medical	$
Recreation	$
Entertainment	$
Total Expenses	$
Profit (Total Income—Total Expenses)	$

Young College Students: Some young adults in college these days get together and buy a house which they can turn around and sell in four years when they are getting ready to graduate. Someone I know bought a house with his room mate in their sophomore year and they sold the house when they graduated and pocket fifty thousand dollars profit. What a smart way to start life after graduation? But not all young adults are smart and responsible enough to make this kind of move.

RETIRE HAPPY

It is all about your nest egg

Retirement Planning

Many people always ask how they can start investing for retirement. You can start by finding out if your company offers a 401K or 403B plan and if they match the contribution. This is dollar cost averaging investment, which you can do through your employer and you can also do it on your own if you have a personal mutual fund account, stock account or any other investment account. Dollar cost averaging is when you make contribution every pay period to an account either by writing a check yourself or through direct deposit solely for investment purposes. Save as much as possible and diversify your portfolio with a 401(k) or similar thrift plan, stocks, CDs, mutual funds, and IRAs—and buy U.S. Savings Bonds. They add up big overtime. With compound interest, there are some retirement accounts like ROTH IRA that if you set up with $20 a week ($1,040 a year) for twenty-five years, with a 5 percent return, you can end up with $50,000.

Pension Plans

Direct Contribution: These are the pension plans most company go by these days e.g. 401K, 403B, 457 plan, salary reduction plan, employee stock ownership plans (ESOP's) and it is usually refer to as DC pension plan. This plan set-aside (or allow you to set aside) a percentage of your salary or a portion of company profits, and the money is put into a retirement account controlled by you. This percentage, you set aside might be foxed or you can choice to fluctuate your set aside as long as you are within the allowed percentage. Your nest egg will depend on how your money earn or grow. This money grows untaxed until you withdraw at retirement. You bear the risk, in case your money did not grow.

Define Benefit: This is the type of retirement plan most companies used to go by and it is refer to as DB pension plan.

A worker with a DB pension plan may have had financial security after retirement, but the worker had no real asset base to pass on to his or her heirs. For example, if a worker retire at sixty-five and died at seventy-five, his benefits often ceased and the investment assets remained with the company he or she used to work for. By utilizing a DC pension plan, if a worker passed away at age seventy-five and there was still something left in his or her portfolio, then the remaining assets in the retirement plan would be passed on to the family member or heirs.

Define benefit plans guarantee to pay you a specified amount when you retire and this is based on your salary, age and years in service. This is backed by a government insurance agency called Pension Benefit Guarantee Corporation (PBGC). About 40 million Americans are covered by defined benefit pension plans. Most of these kinds of plans are really designed so that the pension benefit you receive plus social security benefits will be about 60% to 70% of what you were receiving before you retire.

To calculate the define benefits:

Calculate your final average monthly earnings multiply by 1.5% multiply by years of service = Monthly benefit.

What to know when you no longer work for that Employer.

1. **You can take cash distribution:** This is a very costly option, because your former employers will with-hold 20 percent of the money. And if the money is not rolled over to tax deferred retirement account is subject to Federal tax and some State may also tax this early withdrawal. If you take the cash before age fifty five, you will get 10 percent penalty.

2. **IRA Rollover:** You can roll it over into an IRA rollover account. This is the best option as far as I am concern, because you don't want to take cash distribution while there is compounding interest ahead and you pay 20 percent penalty. You will control the investment. You could even trade stocks, bonds, and options in this account.

3. **Leave the money in your former employer's care:** You can do this if you are happy with the performance, they cannot force you to take the money

if it is more than $5000. You can still direct the investment but not borrow against it, since you no longer work for that employer.

Some employer or your new employer might make you wait for a year before you can participate in their chosen plans. You can roll it to an IRA account temporarily, and then roll it to the new employer. These are the different breakdown

- 401K for corporate
- 403b for community own ventures like Hospitals
- 457 plan for public school system

Trust

The American college Dictionary defines trust as "that on which a person relies; the condition of being confided to another person's care or guard." In Financial terms—a trust is an arrangement that separates the legal ownership of an asset from the entity or person benefiting from that asset. You can open a trust account with your bank, most financial institutions, some insurance or life insurance companies and even some brokerage firms.

Probate: This is the administering of will by the court. Many people seek to avoid this because it is a public record. It is slow, long and a tedious process. The fees to the attorney and executors can mount up. If you own properties and homes in other states, than the state you live in, there will be an ancillary probate.

Living Trust: This (revocable) or living trust can allow you to bypass the probate process. It allows you to manage your assets as if you were still alive. "For example, a gay partner may be well served by a living trust, since this kind of relationship is not legally recognized; a will could be challenged, while a trust is much more difficult to dispute."

The bypass trust: This is the most frequently used trust. Within this trust, there can be living or testamentary, revocable or irrevocable trusts. Irrevocable trust is more favorable with tax treatment. "Married couples most commonly include this trust in their wills to leave the full amount of unified credit (up to $2 million to 2006) to their heirs free of estate tax. Jointly owned property must be divided before death to provide at least the unified credit amount in each spouse's name. When the first spouse dies, the designated assets go into the trust, but the surviving spouse is entitled to income and principal from it at the trustee's discretion. When the second spouse dies, the heirs receive the proceeds of the trust free of estate tax. About $2 million is sheltered from estate tax."

Credit Shelter trust: This is also called a bypass trust. This is for estates that have over $625,000 exemption. "Credit shelter trusts allow you to leave the highest amount of money that can go free of taxes to the trust when you die so that it doesn't go to the spouse and thus avoids taxation in spouse estate."

A qualified terminal interest trust: This is also called Q-tip trust. This trust is used mostly often by people who have children from previous marriages and want to be sure that they are taken care of.

A dynasty trust: "This trust is often established as generation-skipping trust, which uses the exemption from the tax on the transfers that skip over a generation."

Charitable Reminder Trust (CRT): This is a good instrument for a grantor who wants to benefit a charity by donating assets that have appreciated sharply during his or her lifetime. If your dad has stocks that have appreciated sharply and want to have enough income to pay his bills and also leave some for his alma mater. This type of trust may be his best bet.

Gifts: This is a very good way for the rich to avoid estate taxes, because if the estate is up to $625,000 or more, the Federal estate taxes kick in. It will increase to $1 million by 2007. If you give someone or your love ones like your children $10,000 gift per a year, the money will be exempted from Federal taxes. If you are married, you can elect to gift-split with your spouse and raise the tax-free limit to $20,000. If you give to one person more than $10,000 in a year, only the first $10,000 is tax-exempt. Another way to do it is by paying for your grand children's private school or college education. You can really use gifting to distribute your assets and avoid high Federal estate taxes.

Irrevocable Trust: Irrevocable life insurance trust purchase life insurance policies on individuals and the premiums are paid directly by the trust or by the future beneficiaries on behalf of the trust. This is for example; one million dollars in life insurance trust bypass the probate and is not taxed in the individual's estate.

Support Trust: This trust is designed to support your children and your spouse. It can be set up detailing how the income and trust principal should be distributed. "The trustee can be given flexibility or not depending on the situation." This is discretionary trust. For example if you want your money to be invested for a child's education, it can be done. You also can arrange for your children to take loans against the trust to put down as payment on a house.

WILL

Having a will is very important. This is because it is better for you to make the decision about how you will like to distribute your things before you pass on. You don't have to be rich to make a will. It is very important because, you don't want your worst enemy to be fighting over your things after you pass on. You make a will privately, or have a lawyer help you to make one. If you do it by yourself with do-it-yourself kit, don't forget to have it witnessed and you sign it.

Durable Power of Attorney: It allows a person to act on your behalf in all matters if you are mentally or physically unable to make decisions.

Pour-Over Will: "This would allow anything you've bought but haven't had time to record in the trust to be automatically included at the time of death."

A Living Will: It is your instructions on what to do if you become mentally or physically incompetent or for example if you don't want to be kept alive on a respirator or if you prefer to be cremated rather than been buried.

People Power: You need an executor and if possible a co-executor to make sure your wishes is carried out.

Life is what you do while waiting to die—What are you doing with your life?

Estate Planning

You use estate planning to avoid taxes and probate court. This is to make sure your money from a life insurance policy or retirement plan end up with the beneficiary of your choice. "Insurance policies and retirement plans are specifically designed to allow an easy transfer of assets to dependents and survivors." "Assigning beneficiaries is something people often do their first day on the job when they are going over benefits with a new employer and they don't realize the importance of their choices."

The drawbacks in assigning beneficiaries

1. Don't name your estate as a beneficiary because it can undo certain policy or retirement plan advantages. Take for example, insurance benefits are generally not subject to claims from creditors, but an estate can be. If your estate is the beneficiary, your insurance benefits may no longer be exempt. As such naming an estate as beneficiary will result in the liquidation of an

individual account upon your death, with taxes becoming due immediately. This can prevent a surviving spouse of continued tax free growth of that money.

2. Some people fail to name a secondary beneficiary in case their primary beneficiary dies. If the primary beneficiary dies before they do, or at the same time, and they have not named a secondary beneficiary, the insurance policy or retirement plan will bounce back to the estate. In this kind of cases, the money will be distributed according to the will or, if they have no will, according to your state's laws.

3. Some people name their minor children as beneficiaries. In most cases, insurance companies, pension plans, and retirement accounts will not pay death benefits to minors. The benefits are held until a court-approved guardian or trustee is appointed. If you want to provide for minors, name a trustee or establish a trust. If you fail to do this, it means the court will name one for you.

4. Some fail to see the tax consequences. Many people have mistaken belief about what is and isn't taxed. Life-insurance benefits are generally free from federal income tax. Regarding tax-deferred accounts, spouses are the only party that can continue to defer taxes in tax-deferred accounts.

Social Security

Social Security was created after the great depression to ensure that seniors were taken care of. Every employee makes FICA payment which is deducted from the employee check. Both the social security and Medicare are deducted from your paycheck at a rate of 7.65 percent. 6.2 percent goes to your social security, while the remaining 1.45 percent goes to Medicare. The self-employed pay their own social security taxes when they pay their income taxes. The IRS then turns around and reports the earnings to social security. The amount an employee pays into social security and Medicare is usually matched by the employer. If you are self employed, you will pay yours and match it. In other words, you pay your rate and match it. The amount you match as an employer is tax deductible.

Social Security Credit Basis

Social security as it is today is calculated on a "credit" basis. It varies for people who work part-time or did not work at all for a whole year. If you earn at least

$700 in a quarter, you earn a credit. The credit rises as you earn above $700. In other words the credit rises as the average income the person earn increases.

Social Security Benefits

If you are born after 1929, you need at least 40 credits to qualify for retirement benefits. And if you were born before 1929, you will need one credit less per a year. Those people that were born after 1959 will need to be at the age of 67 years to obtain full benefit from the social security administration. If you are a widow, you may be eligible to receive survivor's benefits if you are at least 60 years old. The unmarried widows or widowers raising a child entitled to child's benefits may receive the mother's or the father's benefits. The people or anybody of any age working or worked, who had received a steady income of at least $500 per month or a certain number of credits accrued depending on age, can receive social security disability payments if they become unable to work for an extended period.

If you need your personal earnings and benefit estimate statement, contact the social security Administration and request for form SSA-7004. You can contact the Social Security Administration online at: www.ssa.gov or socialsecurity.gov

The Address is:
P. O. Box 17743
Baltimore, MD 21235
Phone # 1-800-772-1213.

You can request for a copy of your personal Earnings and Benefit Estimate Statement at least every five years to be sure that your money is intact. If you look at your paycheck and your employer did not deduct your social security contribution, you should remind your employer.

The Medicare

Medicare information can be given to you by Social Security office. The Medicare system provide the basic health care insurance to people who are 65 years of age and over who are entitled to Social Security benefits, whether they are receiving the Social Security benefits or not. They also provide the same assistance to disabled people receiving Social Security disability payments for at least two years. The people who require kidney dialysis or a kidney transplant may be eligible for Medicare at any age regardless.

You can contact Medicare at:
Medicare.gov or hcfa.gov

Phone# 1-800-772-1213

What age will you receive full benefit?

Birth Year	Age in Year	Plus Months
Pre-1938	65	+0
1938	65	+2
1939	65	+4
1940	65	+6
1941	65	+8
1942	65	+10
1943–54	66	+0
1955	66	+2
1956	66	+4
1957	66	+6
1958	66	+8
1959	66	+10
1960 and after	67	+0

How do they figure out your benefit payments?

This is based on the amount you and your employers have paid into Social Security. This is because you earn credit for Social security benefits for each quarter (3-month period) that you work. And earn at least $890, and pay FICA taxes. You do not lose credits if you change jobs or have gaps in employment. But if you were born in 1929 or later, you need 40 quarters (10 years) of coverage to be eligible for Social Security retirement or disability benefits.

Americans that receive Social Security

It is reported that more than 46 million Americans receive retirement or disability benefits, and about 155 million workers pay Social Security taxes. Medicare hospital insurance covers about 30 million Americans over 65 years. All these numbers may change as baby boomers start to exit the workforce. I mean those born between 1946 and 1964.

Social Security Collection and guideline

- You can start receiving social security benefits early at 62, but the longer you wait, the higher your monthly benefit will be. You get docked five—ninths of one percent for every month you are younger than 65. This is about 20% less per month.

- The maximum social security benefits range from $1,422 per month for someone who retires early at 62 to $2,111 for someone who retires at age 70.

- Social security benefits are not automatic. You have to apply before you can start collecting. Most cases, according to the social security administration, it is better to schedule an appointment three months before your retirement date.

- You can contact them by calling 1-800-772-1213 and you can also apply over the internet at http://www.socialsecurity.gov. And you will eventually need to go to their office to complete the process. They will need you to show a proof of age. They prefer birth certificate.

- If you need information about applying for social security benefit, you can get it at their web site—http://www.ssa.gov or call their number for a brochure.

How Medicare Cover Patients

The Medicare System covers both medical and hospital stay insurance. The Medicare first part of the coverage is known as part B. The medical insurance covers:

- The doctor's fees
- The physical therapy
- The x-rays
- The diagnostic tests

The other part is the hospital insurance portion which is part A. The hospital part of the insurance covers the hospital stay and could include a skilled nursing facility after the individual had stayed in the hospital. You should know that you can have the Medicare portion of your Social Security sent straight to your HMO or Health Management Organization that you may be using as your provider.

Working and collecting social security

If you apply after you are due, you will get back payments up to six months. If you work and collect Social Security after the age 65, the government will take away $1 of your Social Security benefit for every $3 you earn over certain earned-income limits. In 1995 the limit for people ages 65 to 69 is $11,280, and for those ages 62 to 64, is $8,160. (The limits go up each year by the same amount as Social Security benefits.) The maximum you can get back from Social Security as in 2004 is $21,900 a year. Once you are 70, you can earn as much as you want from your job and still collect your full Social Security benefits.

The flip side of social security

The government can take certain amount of your check every pay period toward social security without your say so (or giving them permission). And the money is used to pay social security to the elderly, Medicare, section eight and many other social programs. The fund is not invested and it is always in deficit. The government on the other hand can turn around and tell you when you are sixty-four and getting ready to start collecting social security that you cannot collect until you are seventy or they can say that the program is cancelled that you will not get anything back at all. The money is not invested anywhere at all to be generating interest. It is always spent like a poor working fellow from hand to mouth. If a private company come up with the same kind of program that emulate the social security, just like your employer does—taking out the money that will provide you with so call death benefit, Medicare etc. The government will require them to put the money in an interest bearing account; if not the company officers will be prosecuted and put in jail. A company in Texas came up with a plan that mirrors the social security system, i.e. taking out the same amount (that the government is taking out) every pay period and investing the money in interest generating account. They concluded that when you retire, you will be withdrawing three times what you were making when you were working. Are politicians in Washington really helping us? I personally think that social security should be invested like your 401(k)—Should be invested in an account that protect your principal—in that it will generate interest and if you die, your family can get the money. Many countries are already doing this successfully. Social security as it is now is that America government is stealing by tricks from its hard working citizens. Politicians want to have a container that they can easily dip into for their extravagant spending and lifestyle without any accountability. The social security fund is a poor investment fund because of what it generates or due to what we get back. We need a better social security fund.

> *Have you ever wondered how some of the America's greatest fortunes were made? They were made, in large part, by the magic of compound interest......Today, the same principle is at work in your individual retirement accounts and your company retirement plans.*

> —James Jorgensen, It's never too late to get Rich.

Types of Retirement Plan

Keogh Plans: Keogh are mostly popular with people who are self employed. A self employed individual is allowed a maximum contribution of $30,000 per year. Actually in Keogh plan, employers set aside money for themselves and their employees. Employees are eligible for coverage after working 1,000 hours or more per year for three years.

There are three types of Keogh plans:

1. **Profit Sharing Keogh:** In this plan, annual contributions are limited to 15 percent, but can be as low as 0 percent in a given year.

2. **Money Purchase Keogh:** In this plan, annual contributions are limited to 1 to 25 percent of the compensation. And once it is set, it must continue for the life of the plan.

3. **A paired Keogh:** This plan combines the terms of profit sharing and money purchase plans.

    Generally, Keogh plans are suppose to be established by December 31st of the year for which you want to start making contributions, you have until you file your tax return to make the contribution. And if you file an extension, you have until October 15th.

    Just like the IRA's, 401(K) and 403(b) plans, Keoghs have penalties for early withdrawal, or money taken out of the account before the age of 59 1/2. When you finally retire, you can have the money paid to you in monthly amounts or in one lump sum and they are taxable. Distribution must start by age 70 ½.

Basic or Traditional IRA:—Taxes deferred till retirement

A tax payer can contribute $4,000 per person, per year, or 100 percent of earnings up to $4,000, whichever is less. This contribution is a deduction from gross income, thus reducing your personal income taxes. It is deductible really if not done by your employer. But if you and your spouse are covered by an employer plan, you still may be entitled to a partial deduction depending on who is covered base on your adjusted gross income level. Since this is a tax-deferred compounding, tax deductible contribution, you are eligible to contribute if you are under 70 ½ with earned income and your nonworking spouse is also eligible. This is why an IRA is really called an individual plan. The growth i.e., interest, dividends and earnings of the account is not taxed until an individual withdraw the money at retirement. The individual must begin withdrawal at age 70 ½. If the individual withdraw prior to age 59 1/2, he or she is subject to 10 percent penalty tax, unless if he or she withdraw it for or as:

1. A qualified first-time home buyer and the limit should be $10,000.

2. for higher education

3. for medical expenses that exceed 7.5 percent of his or her adjusted gross income.

4. To pay for certain health insurance premiums while unemployed.

5. To pay for series of substantially equal periodic payments that meets special requirements

6. Distributions related to divorce proceedings.

7. Disability

8. Death.

Roth IRA—Tax free distribution at retirement

A Roth IRA is similar to a traditional IRA, except the original contribution of $4,000 per a year is not deductible. The growth of this account is not taxed when money is pulled out at retirement. The compounded earnings will not be taxed. You can contribute to this account if you earn below the limit of $95,000 for single filers and $150,000 for joint filers. In other words, contributions are phased out for individuals with an adjusted gross income between $95,000 and $110,000 and married taxpayers when they reach $160,000. You must withdraw at age 70 ½.

There are no taxes if you own the account for at least 5 years by age 59 ½. No taxes if you withdraw it toward your home as a first-time home buyer at the age of 59 ½ or if you are disable or dies.

"You cannot contribute $3,000 annually to both Roth and a traditional IRA. What you contribute to one reduces the amount that can be contributed to the other. The $3,000 is aggregated among all IRA's."

401 (K)

This is a form of retirement plan that can be set up through an employer or when you own your own business. This is the most common employer plan today. This allows the employees who choose to participate to contribute about 10 to 20 percent of gross income into this investment container. You have to select how you want your money to be invested by the investment firm. *Some employers match the contribution partially or in full.*

The amount that is set-aside is not subject to income taxes. The contributions are 100% vested. The employee can take their contribution if their employment ends with the company. Since up to certain percentage is match by some employers, the taxes to this contribution will take place when the money is withdrawn. An employee can contribute maximum amount of $10,000 per year.

403 (b)

403(b) used to be the only retirement game in town. It was for teachers, hospital workers, and non-profit workers. They use the money to buy insurance company annuities. They did not have choices to compare the performances of this investment program.

Today an employee can transfer a sluggish 403 (b) into 403 (b) (7) custodial account at a brokerage firm or a mutual fund company, where they can invest in any mutual fund or annuities they wish.

"Be careful: Since most annuities let you withdraw only 10% of your balance without triggering surrender fee, your transfer into a 403 (b) (7) may have to be made gradually."

SEPs

Self employed individuals and small businesses use—Simplified employee Pension (SEP) as retirement plan. This is simple group of IRA's. This is because all qualified employees simply set up an IRA account to which the employer will make contributions. These are made at a rate of 15% of the employee's salary, with a maximum contribution of 24,000. This is simple and has less paperwork.

SIMPLE IRA PLAN

This is called a savings incentive match plan for employees or SIMPLE. This can be initiated by self employed individuals or employers with 100 or fewer employees. It works like 401 (K) plan. Certain portion of the employee salary is contributed into the retirement plan. An employee can contribute a maximum of $6,000 per year, while the employer can match the contribution up to 3% of the employee salary. This contribution is not taxed.

SARSEP—A 401 (K) substitute for small business

This is a salary reduction and simplified version of 401 (K) plan. In this case, for example, you are a small business owner with 25 employees or fewer than 25. In this plan, you can start for yourself and your employees by making contributions to yours and their retirement accounts through salary reduction. What the business do, is to set up the individual retirement accounts for those employees who want to join the program. There is a limit as to how much contribution that can be made to this account. It is limited to 13% for employer and 15% for the employees and in either case not more than $9,240. This is how it was in 1995. It must have changed by now. If you are interested, consult your financial adviser. The employees are free to choose how much they want to contribute and they can stop or change the amount anytime they want.

If your employees contribute an average of 5% of their pay, your percentage contribution would be limited to 6.25%.

412 (i)

If you are behind on your retirement savings, the IRS Tax code 412 (i) is a very good way to catch up. This is a deferred-benefit plan that lets businesses make super sized contributions in exchange for a guaranteed retirement income for the owner and employees. This plan has been around since in the 1970's.

A business can contribute between $100,000 and $300,000 a year. The amount varies depending on the age, incomes and years of service of the person. There are about 50 insurance companies that offer this plan. The money will only be invested in whole insurance and annuities with a set return of 2% to 4% that is guaranteed by the insurance company. You cannot switch to stocks. Administrative fee could be between $1,000 to $2,500 annually. If you have five or fewer employee and you are a conservative investor, this kind of retirement plan might be good for you. Companies like AIG, Mass Mutual and Pacific Life all offer this plan.

457 Plan

A 457(b) plan is a non-qualified tax-deferred compensation plan that works very much like other retirement plans such as the 403(b) and 401(k). Created in 1978 the name refers to the relevant section [457] in the Internal Revenue Code that governs the plan. Two main types of 457 plans exist: governmental and tax-exempt 457(b) plans.

- The plan restricts participation to individuals who work for a state or state subdivision or certain tax-exempt non-governmental organization.

- The maximum amount of compensation that an employee can generally defer under a 457 plan in 2003 is the lesser of $12,000 (increasing $1,000 each following year to $15,000 in 2006, then increasing only for cost-of-living adjustments) or 100 percent of the employee's compensation.

- The plan must provide that a deferral for a given month will not be made unless an agreement has been entered into before that month begins.

Advantages

It reduces your current income taxes while boosting your retirement savings.

It allows earnings to accumulate tax-deferred.

It offers portability—Public (governmental) plan money can be moved into a new employer's 457(b), 403(b) or 401(k) if the plan accepts such transfers, or into an IRA.

Rollover Restrictions

- The expanded rollover provisions do not apply to 457 plans maintained by nongovernmental tax-exempt organizations because, unlike government 457 plans, they are not allowed to hold assets in trust for employees.

- Although the 457 rollover provisions may have been liberalized, the amended rules *do not require* qualified plans, 403(b) annuities, or another 457 plan to accept rollovers. (A rollover to an IRA, though, is still always an available option.)

Borrowing from your retirement accounts

Borrowing from your 401K, 403b or profit sharing plan can allow you to pay off your higher interest debts without paying penalties or fees. You are usually allowed to borrow up to 50% of your account. The maximum in dollar amount is up to $50,000 and the interest can be 1% or 2% above the prime interest rate. If you want to be updated with the rate, you can always check out bankrate.com or banx.com. Usually the IRS expects this kind of loan to be paid back in five years. If the loan is used to purchase a home, that happen to be your primary resident, you do not have to pay it back in five years

IRA money can be used interest free if you roll the IRA into "roll over IRA" and pay it back within 60days. If you cannot pay it back within 60 days, you will pay penalty and taxes on the money. There is no credit check if you want to borrow from your IRA or retirement plan. You will be paying yourself interest and not earning return on your money from someone else. This is really a bad deal, because you will be paying yourself less interest than you can make from the retirement account. If you fail to make payments, you will pay 10% penalty plus taxes. If you leave your job, the entire loan is due and most employers don't allow former employees to repay in installments. There is also double taxation here too, because you are paying the loan back with after tax money and this money will be tax at the time you will withdraw the money.

ANNUITY

A tax favored investment that generates a series of regular payments guaranteed to continue for a specific time (usually the recipient's lifetime) in exchange for a single payment or a series of payments.

Deferred Annuity: Payments begin sometime in the future

Immediate Annuity: payments begin immediately

Fixed Annuity: pays a fixed income stream for the life of the contract

Variable Annuity: The payments may change according to how successfully the money is invested.

Annuity is a good protection:

- If you are afraid of a lawsuit because most states protect at least some assets that are held in annuity from creditors.

- If you do not have retirement savings or just have little retirement savings and you need a steady monthly income.

These companies will provide you with a free information packet for annuities:

- Jack White—1-800-622-3699

- T. Rowe Price—1-800-469-6587

- Ameritas No-Load—1-800-552-3553

- Jack Hancock—1-888-742-6262
- Schwab Variable Annuity—1-800-838-0650
- USAA—1-800-531-6390

If you want to buy variable annuity in your IRA account, you should know that annuities are tax deferred.

PAYING FOR YOUR CHILDS COLLEGE

The definitive guide on paying for college can be found when you read "Paying for college without Going broke by Kalman Chang" This book dispels the myths about financial aid and tells you how to maximize costs by maximizing your child's eligibility for financial aid and how to negotiate for more aid, and what are the best loan programs available.

Note: If your children have college saving plans like 529 and educational IRA's, they might not qualify for financial aids, like the free money not the loans. Seek other options like I or EE bonds or regular saving account.

PRE-PAID TUITION PLAN (529)

Prepaid tuition plan is where most parents can pay in advance the tuition for their kids over many years for an education at a school in their state or other state. This tuition saving plan is state sponsored savings plan for college education. But you need not invest in your home state. You should check with your state of residence or the state in which your college of choice is located. The money you put in this plan are tax-deferred until you use them for college. If you withdraw early before the child is eligible for college, there will be a substantial penalty. These plans have different management and in some states, you may deduct your contribution on your state taxes. You will be taxed on the funds when you withdraw the money from the plan.

What program is right for you?

1. Check with your state first
2. Check the different investment options
3. Check out the fee they charge
4. Check out if your employer offer this plan
5. Check out Coverdell account

Educational IRA

The educational IRA was created in 1998 and it now allows a contribution of $4,000 per child per a year. The child that this IRA is set-up for must be under 18 years of age. This child must have his or her contribution made to a qualified state tuition program. You can withdraw your contribution from this program tax free to offset education costs, including tuition, books, room and board. Your income should not exceed $95,000 for individuals or between $190,000 and $220,000 for couples. The education IRA does not preclude Roth IRA—You or your spouse and your child can contribute to both Roth and Education IRA at the same time.

If your child did not use the money: You can transfer the whole or part to another child under 30. Once your child turns 30, it must be distributed. If the student makes withdrawal other than for educational purpose, the earning will be included in your child's gross income. Apart from it been included in the gross income, it will be taxed 10% and it is subject to a 10% penalty.

> *"If you want to have hope of getting financial aid, avoid education IRA's, Roth IRA's or Regular IRA's in your children's name—UGMA and UTMA accounts, and all prepaid tuition plans. You're better off keeping the funds in your name."*
>
> —*Kalman Chany*

UGMA and UTMA

The UGMA and URMA mean "The Uniform Gift to Minors Act and the Uniform Transfer to Minors Act (only one applies in each state) are designed to make it easy to give gift (securities) to minors. Each parent can gift as much as $10,000 per year to a UTMA or UGMA under the acts provisions, the minor is the owner of the securities, but a parent or legal guardian acts as custodian of the child's money, responsible for prudently investing assets until the child reaches maturity, either 18 or 21, depending on your state."

Tax advantages of UGMA and UTMA

There is a lot of tax savings in this account. You should know that the first $700 of unearned income in a minor's account is exempt from tax, regardless of his or her age, while the second $700 of unearned income is taxed at the minor's rate. "At age 14, all income greater than $700 is taxed at the child's own rate, 15 percent for income, and 10 percent for capital gain."

You should know that assets in UTMA and UGMA accounts can interfere with your child's ability to qualify for financial aid. The amount that your child qualifies for depends on your family's expected contribution. Your child portion is 35 percent of his or her assets and half of his or her annual income over $2,400 and the more assets in the child's name, the more difficult it will be for the child to qualify for financial aid.

"Parent's must contribute a maximum of 5.65 percent of their assets to tuition before the student qualifies for need based financial aid. Assets in tax deferred accounts, like 401 (K) or other retirement plans, annuities, and cash values of insurance policies are generally excluded from these calculations of parents' expected contributions." "Looking for financial aid for your kid? Common sense will tell you it is best to keep the money in your name so you do not disqualify your child, right? If you are in the top tax bracket, think again. Since you probably won't qualify for any need based aid programs, you may as well put the money in your kid's names." You can get free brochure—borrowing for college at (1-800-891-4595).

TERM LIFE

Always remember that life insurance is for the living, not for the dead. You need life insurance, if you have dependent, so that they will not suffer if you die accidentally or naturally.

Term life offers the most coverage for the lowest cost. All you have to do is pick a number mostly between $50,000 to $500,000 or more and pay the annual premium. If you die while you own this kind of policy and making your payments up to date, your beneficiaries will get paid. "Term life is simple insurance—This is death coverage, pure and simple, with no bells and whistles involving savings plans or complicated investments. For identical death benefits, term premiums are generally one-quarter to one-tenth the size of cash-value premiums."

The premium they expect you to pay is based on the amount of insurance you need, your general health and your age when you first purchase the insurance. The insurance will rise as you grow older. In some policies, the premium rise every year while some are fixed for about five year period. As long as you are paying your premium, you can have a guarantee renewal in most policies. And you can buy a non-renewable term policy, until your children finish college. As in 1994, the five companies with the best dividend Payment record after a policy has been surrendered after 20 years were

• Guardian Life

- State Farm
- North Western Mutual
- Country Life
- Phoenix Life

DISABILITY COVERAGE

Disability insurance is income protection insurance and it is very important just in case you become disabled. Although this insurance doesn't pay 100% of your regular income, it does pay a good portion of your regular income. If you rely on earned income, you really need to have this insurance. Most employers have a similar benefit plan, but not the same. It is paid sick leave, but cover to a certain period. If your employer has this kind of benefit, take advantage of it. Some states pay benefits for up to 26 weeks on non-occupational disability and in California, benefits can run up to 52 weeks. You should know that a benefit from an employer's policy is subject to income tax, unlike benefits under a policy you pay for by yourself. Social security includes benefits for long-term disabilities, but the coverage might not be enough.

You should know that when you buy disability insurance, the longer you agree to wait before coverage starts, the lower the cost. Some people might want the policy for a shorter time frame, which will lower the premium—take for example, some people might want it to cover them until they turn 65 years old, when they will fully be eligible for the social security coverage. Another way some people save money is if they buy a policy that is not protected by inflation i.e. the worth of $2,300 today might be $1,500 in ten years, if inflation averages 4% per year.

LONG TERM CARE INSURANCE

Most nursing home cost over $30,000 dollars a year. Remember that Medicare does not pay for long term care in nursing homes; they only cover your medical bills, not the nursing home bills. Although the benefit of this kind of insurance cover the cost of nursing-home care or of care that allows you to stay in your own home. If you buy this insurance earlier, you will save some money. If you wait till retirement age, the premium will be high. According to 12 steps to a worry-free retirement by Daniel Keher, this is what you should look for when buying this kind of policy.

- A prior stay in a hospital should not be required before you collect benefits and coverage for Alzheimer's disease or related disorders should be guaranteed.

- Home care should be included as a regular benefit or available with an extra premium. A policy that allows beneficiaries to alternate between home and nursing home is best.

- Look for at least a partial inflation-adjustment provision.

- The policy should be guaranteed renewable for life.

- The policy should have a "waiver of premium" clause that allows you to make no payments after receiving benefits for a specified time.

- The policy should have a "free look" period. This period allows you to change your mind and cancel the policy at no cost within the first 30 days.

To get a free list of companies offering Long Term Care Insurance, write to: Health Insurance Association of America 555 13th St NW Washington, DC 20004.

Tax Break When You Sell At 55

This is really a big break for homeowners. If you sell your home at 55, you can take $125,000 of your profit from the sale tax-free. According to the 12 steps to worry free retirement by Daniel Keher, here is how you qualify:

1. You or your spouse must be at least 55 years old before the date of the sale.

2. The home must be your principal residence. It could be condominium, mobile home and even house boat.

3. You must have owned and lived in the home three out of the five years leading up to the sale.

You may not want to use this kind of break to shelter a small amount. You cannot use it in one house for example to shelter $75,000 and then in a second home for $50,000. You will be better off if you and your spouse plan it very well and take a full advantage of the $125,000, since you can do this only once.

REVERSE MORTGAGE

If you own a home, then you have a retirement income in the roof over your head. But, it depends on the way you look at it and your responsibility to yourself and your love ones. You have two choices

1. Sell it if you wish and move to a less expensive house, then pocket the difference.

2.   If you turn 62, take out a reverse mortgage and still stay in it.

This kind of move can make you look like you are the banker, when you go to the closing, instead of you paying, they will pay you. The most important thing to qualify for a reverse mortgage is that the elderly owner must own the house free and clear or close to it.

The loan mean you are actually borrowing against the equity on the house, but you don't have to move out of the house:

1.   You can get a lump sum up front

2.   You can choose to receive fixed monthly payment

3.   You can have a line of credit to draw from when you need the money.

If the owner move out for some reason and the loan is more than the sale price, the lenders get the loss. There are conditions, costs, and many other reasons that Feds require potential borrowers to be sent to counseling. If you are interested call—1-800-569-4287.

Advice and Warnings:

"Reverse mortgages carry very high up-front fees. If the loan is held for only a few years, its cost can be extremely high. And because the interest compounds in the bank's favor, the younger you are, the less you'll get. For example, HUD estimates that a 65-year-old can borrow up to 26% of a home's value, and a 75-year-old can borrow up to 39%, while an 85-year-old can get up to 56%. But reverse mortgages may turn out to be a blessing for those whose home is their biggest, and perhaps only, significant asset, who need additional cash for living expenses, and who don't need to leave the home to heirs. For more information, go to www.aarp.org/hecc/home.html or write to AARP Home Equity information Center, 601 E. Street, NW, Washington, DC 20049 and request a free reverse mortgage booklet."

Retirement Readiness

From the Atlanta Journal and constitution, you should make these your checklist when preparing for retirement:

- Decide when you want to retire, what lifestyle you want and how much money that will take.

- Estimate how much investment return—your 401 (K) plan—if your company offers one—will produce each year.

- If your employer provides a pension, determine how much it will pay you.

- Think about where and how you will live.

- Make a budget of expected expenses and income.

- Consider health care costs and potential needs. You'll be covered under Medicare once you are 65 and will have to pay premiums for what's known as part B. That's the coverage for doctors' bills, out-patient care and other services. The premiums will be deducted from your social security checks.

Scams and Schemes

Got you!

Proven scams and schemes that is popular out there today. You have to be careful.

1. **Satellites Sales:** These so call sales people are out there calling people that they happen to be in the neighborhood and they promise you all kinds of premier programs for free. You should really check them out before you sign any contract with them.

2. **Driveway repairers and roof repairers.** Some of these guys are phony and they also pretend that they just happen to be in your neighborhood and that they represent big companies. Make sure you really checkout the company they represent because they might be up to something else.

3. **Sweepstakes Scams:** If you are called for this kind of offer and given the chances to enter sweepstakes or join lottery clubs, often based in foreign countries. Don't respond. If you respond to one of these, you are making yourself a potential victim. They will advise you that you need to pay advance taxes or fees (for attorneys, money transportation, international transfers, money exchange rates)before they send you the check. Then they will ask for the payments in cashier's checks or money orders or wired.

4. **Chain letters:** These letters guarantee you a lot of wealth or riches beyond your belief. They tell you how you can forward the same kind of letter to certain number of people. This is a pyramid rip-off, so don't be fooled.

5. **They promise you a list:** They will send you an e-mail and promise to send you a list of e-mail addresses that you can send bulk e-mail to, for you to be richer. They expect you to pay for the e-mail addresses.

6. **Work at home scams:** Some tells you that you can earn thousands in a day or a week working at home. They want you to send them some money for

the kit. You will not make good money for stuffing envelopes or assembly crafts at home.

7. **Door to door magazine sellers:** You have to be careful with these kinds of sellers, because some of them are not legitimate sellers. They use big company name to make sale subscriptions. You may not get your subscriptions in the mail. Be very careful with door to door sellers of other products.

8. **Postcards and letters:** Be careful with some letters and postcards that ask you for $5 and more for postage and handling for you to receive a so call prize they allege you won or free stuffs.

9. **Credit repairs:** These groups target you if they know that you have a poor credit record and they want an upfront fee. Some of them promise to clean up your credit or they will promise to issue you EIN—(employer Identification number) for you to apply for new credit and start all over. EIN is something you can get yourself if you want to have an employer status.

10. **72 hour credit repair:** This is a Rapid scoring service that is legitimately used by mortgage lenders or brokers with them acting as middle individuals between creditors and credit bureaus. You cannot do this yourself and other companies cannot offer you instant credit repair. This is a scam if anyone tries to offer you this apart from your lender. Even from your lender, you have to be careful.

11. **Vacation promotion and bogus charities:** Most of these calls are quacks and you should be careful not to fall for their rip-off. They are bogus sellers and scam artists.

SCHEMES

◊ Be careful with some multi-level marketing schemes or pyramid schemes that are out there, like selling telephone services, internet ISP services, and many others that will contact you through mail or phone.

◊ Be careful with pre-approved credit cards, because you are not suppose to get the actual card without filling out and signed an application

◊ Be careful with people who charge you fee to help you look for jobs. A real headhunter is not supposed to charge you.

◊ Be careful with instant or quick education, especially on the internet with some ads that says you will need to answer twenty simple questions from a pamphlet to be a certified travel agent or get a degree.

◊ Be careful with many mushroom companies out there who want to re-finance your home.

◊ Some training schools might approach you to come to their office for a job offer and when you get there they start showing you their training programs and class room setups. You should be smart enough to figure out that all they will offer you is training and some loans with job placement promises. This is common for the entry level areas in the Information Technology and Medical fields.

◊ There are direct marketing advising firms out there that might contact you to set up a day trading account with them. This is common in stock, commodity future and currency trading. Do not fall for them, because day trading is dangerous. No one has become rich from day trading.

◊ **125% home equity loan:** Be careful with e-mails, and direct mail that ask you to borrow 125% of your mortgage. When you consolidate credit card debt by taking out home equity loans for more than the value of your house, like 125%, you are asking for trouble. These loans are not like traditional home equity loans that rely on the equity you have built in your home. These loans are not tax deductible and usually they carry very high interest rates. The result is that if you cannot pay they will foreclose on your home or force you into bankruptcy.

◊ **Some furniture sales/rental companies will give you**—The Zero down, Zero interests, Zero payments for one year or even two years. This deal look great, but it is not great at all. At the end of the year or two, you will find out that you owe the payments you have delayed, plus interests. You will be expected to pay much more than the sticker price on what you now have, which is used furniture's or appliances

Car buying schemes:

◊ **The 0 down, 0 interests, 0 payments for one year.** This deal look great, but it is not great at all. At the end of the year, you will find out that you owe the payments you have delayed, plus interests. At the end, you will be expected to pay much more than the sticker price on what you now have, which is used car for sure.

◊ **When you are asked—What you can afford to pay per month?** The salesperson will use your answer base on your payment limit to determine a model they think you can afford, and then recommend the model to you as well as the price they will charge you.

◊   **Arbitration Clause**—After you sign the paperwork for the new car you have just purchased, you are asked to sign an arbitration clause sheet of paper that the dealerships will use to make you waive your right to sue or to participate in a class action lawsuit or to an appeal. If there is a dispute, you agree to present your case to an arbitrator, who will weigh the facts on both sides and suggests a resolution.

◊   **The dealer says they will pay off your old car loan.** Your old debts don't disappear. What you owe on your old car is rolled into the new car price. For example, if you owe $5,000 and the new is $20,000—You will now owe $25,000.

◊   **The dealership may take some points off your credit card scores:** This is for them to make sure you don't qualify for the low-interest loan that was advertised, that made you to come for the car. It could be 0% financing.

◊   Sometimes, the salesperson may tell you to sign the papers for low-interest that drew you to the dealership. About a week later, the salesperson will call you and tell you that you did not qualify for the low-interest. He will tell you to pay more or he will say that you stole the car. (This is a threat)

◊   You go to the dealership and the salesperson tells you that you cannot negotiate the price on the car. They could tell you that this is because they are on sale or special pricing or financing. In fact, most people who disregard what the salesperson says and negotiate save up to $2,000.

Find Free Money and Help

Types of Proposals

1. **A Letter of Intent:** This kind of letter can be two to three pages and it will summarize to the funder a brief description of the project that you want funded.
2. **A letter proposal:** This kind of letter can be three to four pages long. It describes the project plan, the actual request and the company or organization requesting the funds.
3. **The long proposal:** This kind of proposal should include a cover letter, a proposal summary and often it is requested by foundation and government funders.

Grantee

If you are a grantee, you can apply for federal, state, local, municipal and some foundation grants. "All grant funders have published guidelines for the type of grant application that they expect grant seekers to submit. The guidelines generally shadow the funder's review criteria." Most funders don't need a proposal; all they need is for you to fill out their basic application.

For Applications regarding Federal assistant, use standard form 424 and it can be obtained from omb.gov and fill it out if the organization is 501(a), 501(b) or 501(c) nonprofit.

How to write a proposal

You can follow this format to write a proposal letter or a letter proposal.

1. You should state the project's intent upfront.

2. You should explain what your organization does and where services are provided.

3. You should state how the grant monies will be used and what these funds will do for the target population.

4. You should sneak in a little gloom, doom, drama, and trauma (the problem/need).

5. You should show how your proposed program will solve the problem.

6. You should squeeze in the funding period and the number of persons to be impacted.

The keys for grant seeking

*   Know your organization's needs and strength
*   Know your community and its needs
*   Know your potential funders and their goals.

Getting a Grant

Ones you have understood how to write a letter of proposal, you should then match which funder that will meet your needs or your organization's needs. Look for the application or find out if they need a proposal. You should follow up after you send them your letter proposal. If you did not get the grant, do not give up. You should try again.

Money for you

Popular Class action sites: Check these sites out to see if you might be affected or suppose to be a part of a class action. Most of the times the attorney's might not have your information and therefore cannot contact you. Maybe there is some money out there you suppose to claim.

1. www.classactionamerica.com

2. www.classaction.com

You can also checkout this site for Government grants resources, created to help you find, apply for, and receive your government grants fast. Government grants for any purpose.
http://www.governmentgrants.grants.biz

You can Access different grant money from government and foundation agencies. And funding is available for business, personal and more. Easy step by step.
http://www.governmentgrantsnow.com/grantmoney

Enterprise Grants for Minorities: There is a minority business early planning Grant program which offers individual grants for planning and management assistance to minority entrepreneurs and business owners. Grants are to be used to hire professional consultants for feasibility studies, business and management planning, marketing assistance and planning, and/or financial statements and loan packaging—Grants are up to $15,000 with a 25% match being requested. Contact Department of Commerce, 201 W. Washington Ave., Madison, WI 53707—Phone number: 608-267-9550.

Grants to Develop New Technologies for your business: There are grants that you can apply for to acquire new technology for your business from the—(Advanced Technology Program) they work in partnership with industry to foster the development and broad dissemination of challenging, high-risk technologies that offer the potential for significant, broad-based economic benefits for the nation. Types of assistance: Project grants (Cooperative agreements). Estimate of annual funds available: Cooperative Agreements: $209,931,000. Contact: Dr. Lura Powell, Director—Advanced Technology Program, National Institute of Standards and Technology, Gaithersburg, MD 20899—301-975-5187; email Lura.powell@nist.giv: To receive application kit, call ATP customer service @ 1-800-ATP-FUND.

Grants for Science Research: "The office of science Financial Assistance Program provides financial support for fundamental research, training and related activities in the basic sciences and advanced technology concepts and assessments in fields related to energy. Types of Assistance: Project grants. Estimate of annual funds available: $515,000,000. Contact: Grants and contracts Division, office of science, SC-64, Department of Energy, 19901 Germantown Rd, MD 20874; 301-903-5212."

Health Research Grants: "This financial assistance program provides financial support for research, education, conferences, communication and other activities relating to the health of Department of energy workers, as well as other populations potentially exposed to health hazards associated with energy production, transmission and use. Types of assistance: project grants. Estimate of annual funds available: $1,200,000. Contact: office of Epidemiologic studies, Department of Energy, Mail Stop EH-62/270cc, Germantown, MD 20874; 301-903-3721."

Nursing Research Grants: "The National Institute of Nursing Research supports clinical and basic research to establish a scientific basis for the care of individuals across the lifespan—from management of patients during illness and recovery to reduction of risks for disease and disability and the promotion of healthy lifestyles. The types of assistance: Project grants. Estimate of annual funds available: $5,498,000. Contact: National Institutes of Health, Building 45, Room 3AN12, 45 Center Dr, MSC 6300 Bethesda, MD 20892; 301-594-6869."

Money for seniors to fix up or buy a home: "The rural Housing service of the U.S. Department of Agriculture offers special grants through their section 504 program of up to $7,500 if you're over 62, and need to fix up your home. If you have trouble locating your local community development office, Contact National Association of Housing and Redevelopment officials, 630 Eye St., NM. Washington, DC 20001; 201-289-3500 or 877-866-2476."

SSI for Disables and seniors: If you are disables, you can qualify for SSI and if you are 65 and did not qualify for social security benefit, you can qualify for SSI—Supplemental Social Income, and once you qualify for SSI, you automatically qualify for Medicare.—Contact ssa.gov or your local social security office or Contact Social Security Administration, Office of Public Inquiries, 6401 Security Blvd., Room 4C-5 Annex, Baltimore MD 21235; 800-772-1213.

Money to own a Childcare Center: Childcare and development block grant provides money to develop childcare centers and before and after school programs. For more information, contact your state Department of Economic Development or your child care and Development block Grant lead agency.

Arts Grants: "The National Endowment for the Arts (NEA) continues to be the ultimate source of public money for the arts. For the year 200, the NEA gives away $76.6 million in grants." You can reach your regional, state or local organization. Contact the National Endowment for the Arts—1100 Pennsylvania Av., NW, Washington, DC 20506—www.arts.gov. Phone #202-682-5400.

Money for Nursing Students to repay student loans: "This program is designed to increase the number of registered nurses serving designated shortage areas. Nurses can use the money to pay off student loans. Contact Loan repayments programs, Division of scholarships and Loan repayment, Bureau of primary Health care, Health resources and services administration, 4350 East-West highway, Rockville, MD 20857; 301-594-4400; 800-435-6464 or http://www.bphc.hrsa.gov/bhpc or http://www.bphc.hrsa.gov/nhsc."

$2000 Grant to fix up your home: "A family of four can be making up to $30,000 a year and still be eligible. Contact National Association of Community Action Agencies, 1100 17th St., NW, Suite 500, Washington, DC 20036. Phone # 202-265-7546—http://www.nacaa.org."

Free Helps

The Legal services Corporation is set up by Uncle Sam to help low-income individuals in civil matters with legal issues for free. They have offices in many states and have over 6,500 lawyers and paralegals.

Check your phone book or Contact them at—Legal Services Corporation, 750 First St, NE, 11th Fl., Washington, DC 20002; 202-326-8800.

American Bar Association: If you make less than $32,000 a year, you can get a volunteer lawyer for free from this organization. 750 N. Lake Shore Dr., Chicago, IL 60611; 312-988-5000—http://www.abanet.org/legal services

American Civil Liberties Union (ACLU): They have volunteer lawyers and offices all over the country and they handle civil liberty cases for free. "If you feel that your civil liberties have been violated, they may take your case for free. The kind of issues they are most currently working on, include woman's rights, reproductive freedom, workplace rights, AIDS, arts censorship, capital punishment, children's rights, education reform, lesbian and gay rights, immigrants' rights, national security, privacy and technology, prisoners' rights, and voting rights."

Fighting a high Electric or gas bill: "The state utility commissions can help you fight high gas or electric bills. Some will even come out and make sure that your meter is not over charging you. They don't have money to pay for your bills, but they can negotiate payment arrangements with the company for you or suggest non-profit organizations that may have emergency funds to help."

Reduction on your telephone bill: "Link-Up and Lifeline are two government programs that offer up to $84 a year in discounts on your monthly bill and a 50% reduction for your hook-up service, or $30 whichever is less. These programs have income requirements that vary from state to state. Contact your state Utility commissioner's office or Federal Communication Commission. 1919 M Street, NW, Washington, DC 20554; 888-CALL-FCC or http://www.fcc.gov."

Dress for free for success: "Looking for work and can't afford the right wardrobe? There are about 50 non-profit organizations around the country that provide women with two separate outfits for free. One can be used to go to an interview and the other can be used once you get the job. The following organization acts as a clearinghouse for similar opportunities around the country. Bottomless Closet, 445 North Wells, Chicago, IL 60610; 312-527-9664; Fax: 312-527-4305; http://www.bottomlesscloset.org."

Free prescription drugs: You can get any prescription drug free even if you make $40,000. All you need to do is tell your doctor to write a note that you cannot afford it to the manufacturer or call them. You will be picking up your drug once the forms are filled out. "Call the Pharmaceutical Research and manufacturers of America hotline to receive a listing of the drug companies and their programs. Contact Pharmaceutical Research and manufacturers if America, 1100 15th St., NW, Washington, DC 20005; 800-PMA-INFO; http://www.phrma.org."

Free hearing aids: "You can get information on different types of hearing loss, lists of hearing professionals, and information on locating financial assistance for assistive hearing devices by calling The Better Hearing Institute, P.O. Box 1840, Washington, DC 20013; 800-EAR-WELL; www.betterhearing.org."

Free Health Care for Kids: You can make $40,000 and still be able to get free health care for your kids. Children's Health Insurance Program (CHIPS), are in almost any state and they extends medical coverage to many children who may not be covered. A family of four making $50,000 can pay $25.00 a month.

Free eye care for the elderly: If you are 65 and over, you can get free eye care from National Eye care Project. Contact address is—American Academy of Ophthalmology (AAO), P.O. Box 429098, San Francisco, CA 94142; Phone # 415-561-8500 or 800-222-3937; http://www.eyenet.org.

Free eye care: Low income families and kids can get free eye care from VISION USA, by filling out an application on first come basis in January, with treatment following later that year. Contact: VISION, USA—American Optometric Association, 243 North Linbergh Blvd., St. Louis, MO 63141—Phone 314-991-4100 or 800-766-4466—http://www.aoanet.org.

Free Private school for color kids: "A better Chance's mission is to work with minority students from 6th grade through college to open opportunity doors that otherwise would not be open without a helping hand. There are several programs that include helping students receive financial aid for attending private local schools, or summer programs to help prepare for college. Contact: A Better Chance at 419 Boylston St., Boston, MA 02116-3382. Phone # 800-562-7865; 617-421-0965 or http://www.abetterchance.org."

Educational grants

Travel Overseas for Doctorate Research: "This Program provides opportunities for graduate students to engage in full-time dissertation research abroad in modern foreign language and area studies with exception of Western Europe. The program is designed to develop research knowledge and capability in world areas not widely included in American curricula. Money available: $3,141,000. Grants average $22,000. For more information, contact advanced training and Research Team, International Education and Graduate Programs Service, Office of Postsecondary Education, U.S. Department of Education, 400 Maryland Ave., SW, Washington, DC 20202; 202-401-9774; http://www.ed.gov."

Free Money for Ph.D. Students to do research abroad: "Graduate students now have the opportunity to engage in full time dissertation research abroad in modern foreign language and area studies. Contact Karla Ver Bryck Block, Advanced Training and Research Branch, Center for International Education, Office of Assistant Secretary for Postsecondary Education, U.S. Department of Education, 600 Independence Ave., SW, Washington, DC 20202."

Free Money for Foreign Language Degree: "In this global world, foreign languages and international studies are becoming increasingly important. The Department of Education has funds to support centers which promote instruction in foreign language and international studies at colleges and universities. In addition, there are graduate fellowships to pursue this course of study in order to develop a pool of international experts to meet our nation's needs. Funds for centers may be used for instructional costs of language and area and international studies programs, administration, lectures and conferences, library resources and staff, and travel. Grants for fellowships include tuition, fees, and a basic subsistence allowance. Students must apply to those institutions that received the money. For a listing of institutions that received money, contact the office listed below. Students can contact these institutions directly. Money available: Grants: $13,719,000. Contact International Studies Branch, Center for International Education, Office of Postsecondary Education, U.S. Department of Education, Seventh and D Sts., SW, Washington, DC 20202; 202-401-9783; http://www.ed.gov/office/OPE/HEP/iegps/flasf.html."

Free Money for Graduate Students to Study abroad: "Graduate students who would like to spend a year studying overseas can apply for the Fulbright Program, where if accepted, they will receive round trip transportation, tuition, books, maintenance for one academic year in one country, and health insurance. Students apply through the Fulbright program adviser located at their college or university, or they can apply as an at-large applicant by contacting the New York office of the Institute of International Education. Money available: $14,500,000. The average award per student is $21,000, but awards can range anywhere from $1,200 to $40,000."

You can do it yourself

Name Change: "Name change is often for religious purposes, or to have a name which reflects a person's personal beliefs or interests. Many naturalized citizens may change their names to help make English pronunciations easier. All you need to do is fill out a sample form and pay a fee, usually ranging from $35–$200. This is all done through your county probate court, where you must be a resident for at least a year."

Chapter 7 Bankruptcy

You can buy a kit at the store to file for chapter 7 by yourself, or go to the court and get the forms and fill them out yourself.

"Chapter 7 bankruptcy refers to the chapter of the federal statutes (the Bankruptcy Code) that contains the bankruptcy law. Chapter 7 bankruptcy is sometimes called "straight" bankruptcy. This bankruptcy cancels most of your debts; in exchange, you might have to surrender some of your property."

"The whole Chapter 7 bankruptcy process takes about four to six months, costs $200 in filing and administrative fees, and commonly requires only one trip to the courthouse."

"To file for bankruptcy, you fill out a two-page petition and several other forms. Then you file the petition and forms with the bankruptcy court in your area. Basically, the forms ask you to describe:

- your property
- your current income and its sources
- your current monthly living expenses
- your debts
- property you claim the law allows you to keep through the bankruptcy process (exempt property—most states let you keep clothing, household furnishings, Social Security payments you haven't spent and other basic items)

- property you owned and money you spent during the previous two years, and

- Property you sold or gave away during the previous two years."

"Filing for bankruptcy puts into effect something called the "automatic stay." The automatic stay immediately stops your creditors from trying to collect what you owe them. So, at least temporarily, creditors cannot legally grab (garnish) your wages, empty your bank account, go after your car, house or other property, or cut off your utility service or welfare benefits. Until your bankruptcy case ends, your financial problems are in the hands of the bankruptcy court. It assumes legal control of the property you own (except your exempt property, which is yours to keep) and the debts you owe as of the date you file. Nothing can be sold or paid without the court's consent. You have control, however, with a few exceptions, of property and income you acquire after you file for bankruptcy."

"The court exercises its control through a court-appointed person called a "bankruptcy trustee." The trustee is mostly interested in what you own and what property you claim as exempt. This is because the trustee's primary duty is to see that your creditors are paid as much as possible on what you owe them. And the more assets the trustee recovers for creditors, the more the trustee is paid. The trustee goes through the papers you file and asks you questions at a short hearing, called the "creditors' meeting," which you must attend. This meeting is not likely to last more than five minutes. Creditors may attend, too, but rarely do."

"After this meeting, the trustee collects the property that can be taken from you (your nonexempt property) to be sold to pay your creditors. You can surrender the property to the trustee, pay the trustee its fair market value or, if the trustee agrees, swap some exempt property of equal value for the nonexempt property. If the property isn't worth very much or would be cumbersome for the trustee to sell, the trustee can "abandon" the property-which means that you get to keep it. Very few people actually lose property in bankruptcy."

"If you've pledged property as collateral for a loan, the loan is called a secured debt. The most common examples of collateral are houses and motor vehicles. In most cases, you'll either have to surrender the collateral to the creditor or make arrangements to pay for it during or after bankruptcy. If a creditor has recorded a lien against your property, that debt is also secured. You may be able to wipe out the lien in bankruptcy."

"If, after you file for bankruptcy, you change your mind, you can ask the court to dismiss your case. As a general rule, a court will dismiss a Chapter 7 bankruptcy case as long as the dismissal won't harm the creditors. Usually, you can file again if you want to, although you may have to wait 180 days. At the end of the bankruptcy process, most of your debts are wiped out (discharged) by the court. You no longer legally owe your creditors. You can't file for Chapter 7 bankruptcy again for another six years from the date of your filing."

Deeds

Recording a deed is very simple. "Just take the signed, original deed to the land records office. The clerk will take the deed, stamp it with the date and some numbers, make a copy and give the original back to you. The numbers are usually book and page numbers, which show where the deed will be found in the county's filing system. There will be a small fee, probably about $5 to $15 a page, for recording."

A quitclaim deed: It transfers whatever ownership interest you have in the property. It makes no guarantees about the extent of your interest. Quitclaim deeds are commonly used by divorcing couples; one spouse signs all his rights in the couple's real estate over to the other. This can be especially useful if it isn't clear how much of an interest, if any, one spouse has in property that's held in another spouse's name.

A grant deed: It transfers your ownership and implies certain promises—that the title hasn't already been transferred to someone else or been encumbered, except as set out in the deed. This is the most commonly used kind of deed, in most states.

A warranty deed: It transfers your ownership and explicitly promises the buyer that you have good title to the property.

The person who signs the deed (the person who is transferring the property) should take the deed to a notary public, who will sign and stamp it

You should "record" (file) the deed in the land records office in the county where the property is located. This office goes by different names in different states; it's usually called the County Recorder's Office, Land Registry Office or Register of Deeds. In most counties, you'll find it in the courthouse.

Patents and Trademarks:

Patents allow the creator of certain kinds of inventions that contain new ideas to keep others from making commercial use of those ideas without the creator's permission. Trademarks protects distinctive words, phrases, logos, symbols,

slogans and any other devices used to identify and distinguish products or services in the marketplace. "You can file a Disclosure Document with Patent and Trademark Office, and they will keep it in confidence as evidence of the date of conception of the invention or idea."—
Disclosure Document
Assistant Commissioner of Patents
Box DD
Washington, DC 20231
Phone Number—1-800-786-9199 or 703-308-HELP
www.aspto.gov/web/offices/pac/disdo.html

Incorporate your Business: You can file this with the secretary of state office in your state or the state you are trying to incorporate the business. In Georgia, the web site is http://www.sos.state.ga.us. The forms and the instructions are at this web site—search the internet for your state's (Secretary of state's website) or the state that you are interested in and call them if you cannot find it on the web. You will write or fill out an article of incorporation.

Contracts and forms: You can use Quicken—Legal business pro to quickly and easily draw a contract.

Will and estate planning: You can use Will Maker plus by Quicken for easy will writing or get a simple will kit at the office store, like Staple, OfficeMax, Office Depot etc.

Personal Finance software: You can buy MSN Money or Quicken to keep track and manage of your money.

EIN: You can get the application for Employer Identification Number at http://www.irs.gov. The form is SS-4. If you have a home based business in your name, you can obtain an EIN with your name. You don't even have to register your name as a business as long as you are doing business with it at your place of residence. This is completely legal. You should not obtain EIN to work as an employee with it, apart from the fact that it is illegal, your social security contribution will be going to wrong account number. You can simply fill out the form and fax it to the number on the instruction manual. You will get your EIN in no time.

Get Scholarships—Using the web

There are a lot of scholarship programs out there that include blacks and minorities. You don't have to join the military to be able to go to college. No one is going to knock on your door and ask if they can help you with a scholarship.

You have to take the initiative. There is no need for the money to be returned to donating companies because you fail to apply for it.

FAFSA on the Web (Your Key Aid Form & Info)
http://www.fafsa.ed.gov/

FinAid: The Smart Students Guide to Financial Aid
http://www.finaid.org/

Aid & Resources for Re-Entry Students
http://www.back2college.com/

BELL LABS FELLOWSHIPS FOR UNDERREPRESENTED MINORITIES
http://www.bell-labs.com/fellowships/CRFP/info.html

Student Video Scholarships
http://www.christophers.org/vidcon2k.html

Coca-Cola Two Year College Scholarships
http://www.coca-colascholars.org/programs.html

Holocaust Remembrance Scholarships
http://holocaust.hklaw.com/

Ayn Rand Essay Scholarships
http://www.aynrand.org/contests/

Brand Essay Competition
http://www.instituteforbrandleadership.org/IBLEssayContest-2002Rules.html

Gates Millennium Scholarships (major)
http://www.gmsp.org/nominationmaterials/read.dbm?ID=12

Xerox Scholarships for Students
http://www2.xerox.com/go/xrx/about_xerox/about_xerox_detail.jsp

Sports Scholarships and Internships
http://www.ncaa.org/about/scholarships.html

National Assoc. of Black Journalists Scholarships (NABJ)
http://www.nabj.org/html/studentsvcs.html

Saul T. Wilson Scholarships (Veterinary)
http://www.aphis.usda.gov/mb/mrphr/jobs/stw.html

Thurgood Marshall Scholarship Fund
http://www.thurgoodmarshallfund.org/sk_v6.cfm

Presidential Freedom Scholarships
http://www.nationalservice.org/scholarships/

Microsoft Scholarship Program
http://www.microsoft.com/college/scholarships/minority.asp

WiredScholar Free Scholarship Search
http://www.wiredscholar.com
http://www.wiredscholar.com/paying/scholarship_search/pay_scholarship_se arch

Hope Scholarships & Lifetime Credits
http://www.ed.gov/inits/hope/

William Randolph Hearst Endowed Scholarship for Minority Students
http://www.apsanet.org/PS/grants/aspen3.cfm

Multiple Lists of Minority Scholarships
http://gehon.ir.miami.edu/financial-assistance/Scholarship/black.html

Guaranteed Scholarships
http://www.guaranteed-scholarships.com/

BOEING scholarships (some HBCU connects)
http://www.boeing.com/companyoffices/educationrelations/scholarships/

ROTC Military Scholarships (Navy/Army/Marines/Air Force)
http://www.todaysmilitary.com/chart_mil_rotc.html

Easley National Scholarship Program
http://www.naas.org/senior.htm

Maryland Artists Scholarships
http://www.maef.org/

Jacki Tuckfield Memorial Graduate Business Scholarship (for AA students in South Florida)
http://www.jackituckfield.org/

Historically Black College & University Scholarships
http://www.iesabroad.org/info/hbcu.ht

Actuarial Scholarships for Minority Students
http://www.beanactuary.org/minority/scholarships.htm

International Students Scholarships & Aid Help
http://www.iefa.org/

College Board Scholarship Search
http://cbweb10p.collegeboard.org/fundfinder/html/fundfind01.html

Burger King Scholarship Program
http://www.bkscholars.csfa.org/

Siemens Westinghouse Competition
http://www.siemens-foundation.org/

GE and LuLac Scholarship Funds
http://www.lulac.org/Programs/Scholar.html

CollegeNet's Scholarship Database
http://mach25.collegenet.com/cgi-bin/M25/index

Union Sponsored Scholarships and Aid
http://www.aflcio.org/scholarships/scholar.htm

Scholarship & Financial Aid Help
http://www.blackexcel.org/fin-sch.htm

Scholarship Links (Ed Finance Group)
http://www.efg.net/link_scholarship.htm

Scholarships and Fellowships
http://www.osc.cuny.edu/sep/links.html

Scholarships for Study in Paralegal Studies
http://www.paralegals.org/Choice/2000west.htm

HBCU "Packard" Sit Abroad Scholarships (for study around the world)
http://www.sit.edu/studyabroad/packard_nomination.html

Scholarship and Fellowship Opportunities
http://ccmi.uchicago.edu/schl1.html

INROADS internships
http://www.inroads.org/

ACT-SO "Olympics of the Mind" Scholarships
http://www.naacp.org/work/actso/act-so.shtml

Black Alliance for Educational Options Scholarships
http://www.baeo.org/options/privatelyfinanced.jsp

ScienceNet Scholarship Listing
http://www.sciencenet.emory.edu/undergrad/scholarships.html

Graduate Fellowships for Minorities Nationwide
http://cuinfo.cornell.edu/Student/GRFN/list.phtml?category=MINORITIES

Morris Scholarship Search for minority Students
http://www.sciencewise.com/molis

OSAD Scholarships search to study abroad
http://istc.umn.edu/study/scholarships.html

IUPUI Scholarship Database
http://www.iupui.edu/~scentral/

RHODES SCHOLARSHIPS AT OXFORD
http://www.rhodesscholar.org/info.html

The Roothbert Scholarship Fund
http://www.roothbertfund.org/scholarships

Scholarship information service
http://www.freschinfo.com

Financial aid search
http://www.fastweb.com

Fast Aid
http://www.fastaid.com

SallieMae
http://www.scholarships.salliemae.com

EMBARK
http://www.embark.com

GoCollege
http://www.gocollege.com

ExPan Online
http://www.collegeboard.org

CollegeNet
http://www.collenet.com

Internet Security Tips

1. **Virus Protection:** You can install virus protection software's like MacAfee, Norton antivirus etc.

2. **Firewall:** Install a home firewall, because hackers search the internet looking for vulnerable computers to steal credit-card numbers and personal information. Use home firewalls like Black ICE defender or Zone Alarm to drive away these attacks.

3. **Don't send out personal information:** Sensitive information like home phone numbers, addresses, ages should not be sent to strangers on the internet. Do not post pictures on discussion groups without a password access.

4. **Trust a file or sender before you download:** some of the emails, you might receive may contain spy ware.

5. **Dummy email accounts should be used:** Use your primary or original email account for people you trust and friends—consider using free—services accounts like yahoo mail or hotmail to post messages in news-groups

6. **Always check your browser:** Go to browser's preferences menu and delete personal record if there is any or replace them with dummy records. Any website you visit can make permanent record of your visit.

7. **Check the privacy policies of the websites you visit:** Some of these web-sites reserve the right to share you're your information with third parties.

8. **Get cookie crusher:** Cookies are codes stored on your computer that iden-tify you. You can reject unwanted cookies by resetting your browser prefer-ences or use cookie crusher software.

9. **Encrypt sensitive data:** make sure the site is protected before sending credit-card numbers and financial information. Most sites will let you know with a lock display or secure confirmation like "S" in front of http.

10. **Always clean your memory after surfing:** Your computer keeps a log call memory cache of sites you visit. Any one who visits your computer will see all the trail. With cache deleting function in your browser preferences and tool menu, you can get rid of these digital footprints.

11. **Anonymizer:** Sometimes you can use an anonymizer. This will hide your identity. Use sites like—http://www.anonymizer.com

Kids Online Security Tips

◊   Tell your kids to keep their personal information to themselves.

◊   Tell your kids that people may not be who they say they are.

◊   Tell your kids not to open attachments from strangers.

◊   Tell your kids to tell an adult they trust if something online makes them feel uncomfortable.

◊   Tell your kids that meeting online strangers alone is dangerous.

REFERENCES

1. Invest in yourself—Six Secrets to a rich life by Marc Eisenson, Gerri Detweiler and Nancy Castleman. ISBN—0-471-24888-6.

2. 7 Money Mantras for a richer life by Michelle Singletary.

3. Debt—free living by Burkett.

4. ISBN—0-8024-4232-3

5. Slash your Debt : Save Money and secure your future by Gerri Detweiler, Marc Eisenson and Nancy Castleman—

6. ISBN: 0-9659638-3-7

7. 12 Steps to worry—free retirement

8. By Daniel Kehrer

9. Financial Fitness in 45 Days by Lorayne Fiorillo

10. Multiple Streams of Income by Robert G. Allen

11. ISBN 0-471-38180-2

12. Home-Based Business for Dummies by Paul and Sarah Edwards

13. ISBN: 0-7615-5227-9

14. Joe Dominquez and Vicki Robin, authors of—your money or your life.

ABOUT THE AUTHOR

He is the author of *LIVE A HEALTHY LIVE*—He is a straight shooter—This book will cure many financial cancers that plague Americas today. He gives you basic answers to your everyday financial problems. This book will help you move to the next level in your quest to create wealth, gain financial freedom, be debt free, find free money, scholarships/ help and retire happy. He has worked for many fortune 500 companies in retail and Banking businesses.

The author also worked with SunTrust Bank in financial applications—ATM, Teller, Internet Banking, home equity, estate planning etc. The author obtained his first degree in business and went on to obtain M.SC and M.A. He is an Investor, and an educator. He is an authority and a powerhouse when it is time to talk about money. He walks his talk and talk his walk.

INDEX

A

Actors, 1, 99, 108
Autotrade, 14
ARM's Fund, 28
Attitude, 102
A balance sheet, 106
A sample monthly budget, 113
Annuity, 10, 61, 133-134

B

Bonds, 1, 4, 7-8, 10-12, 29, 91, 105, 108, 118-119, 134
Bond funds, 7-8
Blue chip stocks, 13, 15
Buying call options, 19
Buying put options, 19
Be optimistic, 102-103
    Positive and hopeful, 103
Balance Transfer that is tricky, 56
Bankruptcy, 32, 42, 48, 57, 84-86, 143, 152-154
    Your last resort, 85
Business Bankruptcies, 86
Buying too much stuffs, 89

C

Credit cards value, 41
Corporation, 3, 26, 100-101, 105, 108, 119, 149
Certificate of deposit, 5

Classes of funds, The, 9
Class A shares, 9
Class B shares, 9
Class C shares, 9
C-Share annuity, 10
Corporate Bonds, 1, 10
Convertible Bonds, 10
Cyclical stocks, 13
Cheap options trading, 22-23
Combinational options strategies, 24
Creativity, 102
Car loans, 41, 59, 66-67, 79, 82, 94, 96, 99, 112
Credit cards, 37-57, 60, 71, 80-84, 86, 94, 96-97, 106, 109, 111-113, 142
    Choosing a credit card, 45
    The benefits, 51, 123
Cancel your credit card, 50
    The right way, 50
Credit collectors, 53
Credit rating, 37, 49, 55
Checklist, 46, 140
    Before acquiring a credit card, 46
Credit counseling services, 84
Credit cards bill payments, 83
Compound interest, 92-93, 104, 118, 128
Chapter 7 Bankruptcy, 152, 154
Car rental tip, 74
Commodities futures, 35-36

Currency speculation, 36

D

Dollar cost averaging, 14, 118
Dow Jones Industrial average, 16
Drips, 18
Determination and persistent, 102
Disbelieve, 103
Do you owe or own?, 109
Debit cards and ATM Bank cards, 38
Deeds, 30-31, 154
    A quit claim, 27
    A grant, 146, 154
    A warranty, 154
Disability coverage, 137

E

Earned income, 3, 98, 108, 129, 137
EE Bonds, 12, 134
Energy companies, 14
E-commerce and affiliate programs, 33
Execution and action, 102
Employment security, 105, 109
Errors on your credit report, 54
Eliminating your credit cards debt, 81
Exclusions from bankruptcies, 86
Educational grants, 151
EIN, 142, 155
Estate planning, 122, 155, 163
Energy savings, 76

F

Foreclosures, 26, 85
Farmlands, 29
Franchises, 31
Focus, 2-3, 98, 102, 106, 108, 110
Frustration, 103
FICO, 39, 61, 65
Fixing identity theft problem, 55
Factors that causes inflation, 95

G

Growth stocks, 1, 13-14
Getting a grant, 146
Gifts, 32, 43, 121
Gold, 34-35, 46, 49, 51, 73-74

H

HH bonds, 1, 11-12
How to speed up the refinance process, 62
How to spot a bad mortgage lender, 63
How safe is your bet?, 63
Home insurance, 63-64, 72
How the credit card industry works, 44
How to build a good credit, 52
How to increase your credit score, 56
How to cut high cost banking, 90
Hotel securing tip, 74
Hard assets, 34

I

I-bonds, 11
Income stocks, 13-14
Index funds, 16
Internet auction, 32
Income statement, 106, 116
Income and expenses, 106
Investing versus saving, 91
Incorporate your business, 155
IRA Rollover, 119, 132
IRA, 12, 20, 91, 97, 118-120, 128-135
    Basic, 47, 114, 124, 129, 145, 147-148,
        151-152, 163
    Roth, 118, 129-130, 135
International stocks, 18

J

Junk bonds, 11

K

King of money matters, 88
Kids online, 160

L

Lease option, 64
Linear income, 2-3
Leaps, 24
Location and timing, 102
Life is a journey, 113
Lenders may ask, 60
Lenders may not ask, 61
Long term care insurance, 137-138

M

Money market, 6-7, 10, 28, 64, 81, 90-91, 105
   deposit account, 6
   mutual funds, 7-8, 14, 16, 18, 29-30, 34-35, 91, 97, 115, 118
Municipal bonds, 10
Mindset, 101
Meditation, 107

N

No-load, 9, 134
NASDAQ 100 composite, The, 16
Negativity, 103

O

Options, 14, 17, 19-24, 62, 64, 66, 72-74, 81, 106, 119, 134, 158

P

Portable Hobby, 9
Passive income, 3-4, 101
Portfolio income, 3-4, 108
Preferred stock, 17
Pre-foreclosure, 27
Post-foreclosure, 28
Positive enforcers, 101
Passion and desire, 102
Problems and impossibilities, 103
Procrastination, 39, 103
Plan and budget, 106

Play to win, 115-116
Paying off your car loan, 82
Personal bankruptcies, 86
Penny pinchers, 99
Patent and trademarks, 154
Pension plans, 118-119, 123
Pre-paid tuition, 134-135

Q

QQQ option Trading, 23

R

Retirement readiness, 140
Reverse mortgage, 139
Residual income, 1-4, 99
Russell 2000, 16
Reit, 29
   Funds, 7-9, 12, 14, 16, 18, 28-30, 34-35, 64, 89, 91, 95, 97, 106, 115, 118, 134-135, 145-149, 151, 158
   Municipal mortgage, 29
Refinancing your mortgage, 61
Refinancing your car, 67
Rental insurance, 51, 65
Retirement Accounts, 118, 123, 128, 131, 133
   401 (K), 130-131, 136, 140
   403(b), 128, 130, 132
   Seps, 130
   Simple IRA, 131
   SARSEP, 131
   457 plans, 132
   412 (i), 131
   529, 12, 134

S

Stocks, 1, 4, 7-8, 13-18, 20, 29, 35, 91, 108, 114, 118-119, 121, 131
Stock funds, 7-8
Sector funds, 16
S&P 500 composite, 16

Single stock futures, 17

Short sellers, 18

Selling or writing covered call, 20

Secrets of success, 104

Secured credit card, 37

Stolen or lost credit cards, 54

Save, 5, 38, 46, 56, 59, 63, 69-73, 76-77, 79, 83, 88-92, 95, 97-99, 104-105, 111, 118, 137-138, 144, 161

    Savings accounts, 1, 5, 52, 89, 92

Simple interest, 82, 92

SSI for seniors, 148

Scholarships, 70, 148, 155-159, 163

Social security, 52-53, 75-76, 114-115, 119, 123-128, 137, 140, 148, 152, 155

    Benefits, 51, 61, 100, 115, 119, 122-127, 136-138, 147, 153

Scams, 141

Schemes, 141-143

Silver, 34-35, 46, 73-74

T

Treasury securities, 6

    Government securities, 7, 90, 95

Trade option, 21

    Like a professional, 21

Tax forfeited lands, 29

Tax lien certificates, 26, 30

Tax deeds, 31

Triple Net lease real estate, 32

Try to predict the future, 114

The most common long term expense, 59

Title insurance company, 65

The real truth behind credit cards, 42

Trouble with credit cards, 43

Take charge of your credit card debt, 48

Twelve ways to avoid debt, 82

Try to forecast interest rates, 95

Trust, 29, 63, 120-123, 132, 159-160

    Living, 81, 89, 91, 98, 101, 105, 120, 122, 136, 139, 152, 161

    The bypass, 120

    Credit shelter, 121

    A qualified terminal interest, 121

    A dynasty, 121

    Charitable reminder, 121

    Irrevocable, 120-121

    Support, 61, 86-87, 100, 121, 147, 151

The medicare, 124, 126

Term life, 136

Tax break, 80, 138

    When you seel at 55, 138

Termite pest control, 78

Tax tip, 74

U

U.S. treasury bills, 7

Utility companies, 14

UGMA, 135-136

URMA, 135

W

Without dollar cost advantage, 15

Wealth creation scenario, 103

Where is your money going wrong?, 113

What lender may want from you to refinance, 62

What to do to prevent poor mortgage loans, 65

What can make or kill your credit, 39

Ways to make money at your bank, 89

Ways to simplify your finances, 96

Ways to save your money, 69

Will, 3-7, 9-10, 12-14, 16-22, 27-28, 30-33, 35-50, 52-74, 76-86, 88, 90-97, 99, 101-105, 107-108, 110-113, 115, 118-127, 129-146, 149-151, 153-155, 160, 163

    pour over, 122

Living, 81, 89, 91, 98, 101, 105, 120, 122, 136, 139, 152, 161

Y
Young college students, 116
Your rights if credit is denied, 48
Your bank's balance sheet, 110
You can do it yourself, 152

Z
Zero coupon bonds, 11

0-595-33423-7